HARDCORE
WINDOWS® XP

THE STEP-BY-STEP GUIDE
TO ULTIMATE PERFORMANCE

HARDCORE
WINDOWS® XP
THE STEP-BY-STEP GUIDE
TO ULTIMATE PERFORMANCE

Joli Ballew

McGraw-Hill/Osborne

New York Chicago San Francisco Lisbon
London Madrid Mexico City Milan New Delhi
San Juan Seoul Singapore Sydney Toronto

The McGraw-Hill Companies

McGraw-Hill/Osborne
2100 Powell Street, 10th Floor
Emeryville, California 94608
U.S.A.

To arrange bulk purchase discounts for sales promotions, premiums, or fund-raisers, please contact **McGraw-Hill/Osborne** at the above address. For information on translations or book distributors outside the U.S.A., please see the International Contact Information page immediately following the index of this book.

Hardcore Windows® XP: The Step-by-Step Guide to Ultimate Performance

1234567890 FGR FGR 0198765

ISBN 0-07-225865-9

Vice President & Group Publisher	Philip Ruppel
Vice President & Publisher	Jeffrey Krames
Acquisitions Editor	Majorie McAneny
Project Editor	Janet Walden
Acquisitions Coordinator	Agatha Kim
Technical Editor	Tom Dunlap
Copy Editor	William McManus
Proofreader	Claire Splan
Indexer	Claire Splan
Composition	International Typesetting and Composition
Illustration	International Typesetting and Composition
Series Design	Lucie Ericksen, Peter Hancik, Scott Jackson, James Kussow
Cover Design	James C. Korne

This book was composed with Adobe® InDesign® CS.

For all of my teachers, past, present, and future, from my earliest days in the Garland Independent School District to the University of Texas at Arlington to Richland and Eastfield Community Colleges and beyond. Thank you.

⬎ About the Author

Joli Ballew is a full-time writer, Windows expert, and digital media enthusiast who also teaches, creates web sites, and consults from her home base of Dallas, Texas. Joli has written over a dozen books, including *Windows XP Professional – The Ultimate User's Guide* (Paraglyph Press), *Degunking Windows* (Paraglyph Press), and *Windows XP: Do Amazing Things* (Microsoft Press).

In addition, Joli is a Microsoft Windows XP Expert Zone columnist, holds MCSE, MCDST, and A+ certifications, and has a B.A. in mathematics. She teaches FrontPage at her local community college, has written several books on Photoshop and other graphics programs, and assists with artwork for North Texas Graphics, a screen printing and embroidery company.

About the Technical Editor　**Tom Dunlap** is a freelance editor and consultant specializing in technology. He is a former senior editor at CNET.com and his work has appeared on CNET.com, ZDNET.com, and MSN.com, and in the *San Francisco Chronicle* and other publications. He penned 2004's, *How to Do Everything with Your Sony VAIO*, published by McGraw-Hill/Osborne. Tom is based in Cupertino, CA.

Contents at a Glance

Contents

Acknowledgments

Quite a few people participated in bringing this book to life; it takes much more than just a writer to get it done. First, a special thanks to Margie McAneny for selecting me to write it, Agatha Kim for keeping everyone on the same page, and Tom Dunlap for patiently, quickly, and diligently performing the technical editing tasks. Another round of applause is needed for my copy editor, Bill McManus, who painstakingly dotted the i's and crossed the t's, and made sure I didn't go wild with the semicolons, a nasty little habit of mine.

Of course, I want to thank Neil Salkind of Studio B, my agent, who is always there to tell me how great I'm doing, and to offer words of encouragement. Finally, a special thanks to my family—Mom, Dad, Jennifer, and Cosmo—who continue to support me through the harried book writing phase, followed by the "I'll be on the golf course today; I don't have anything to do" phase. It takes some hardcore effort to write, edit, produce, and publish a book, and I had a hardcore team!

Introduction

A hard-y welcome to *Hardcore Windows XP: The Step-by-Step Guide to Ultimate Performance* for all hardcore Windows XP users! If you're a hardcore *user*, this is the book you've been waiting for. Here you'll learn how to enhance the performance of your computer by taking control of everything from screen savers to background applications to group policies. You'll learn many of the tricks the pros know, too, including how to speed up the boot process, how to turn off unnecessary applications and services, and how to use built-in administrative tools like Event Viewer, just to name a few.

This book is for hardcore *readers* too. You don't have to open and read the book from cover to cover. In fact, you should do just the opposite. Want to learn how to work remotely from home? Turn to Chapter 4. Want to find out how to take control of Service Pack 2? Chapter 5. Want to configure account lockout if a user has tried unsuccessfully to log on three or more times? Skip on over to Chapter 11. It's all here—everything you need to know to work faster, smarter, and more securely.

Because the book is a reference manual and not a tome to be read sequentially, the book's chapters are laid out a little differently than other books. In fact, each chapter is completely independent of the others. There is logic behind the madness, though, and the chapters *are* in a logical order. The book starts by showing how to personalize your user interface, moves on to describe how to tweak and enhance performance from the ground up, and continues through controlling the computer and its users with administrative tools and local security policies. So, if you want to do it all and take full advantage of what Windows XP has to offer, follow the chapters in the order in which they are presented; otherwise, skip around to your heart's content.

Throughout the chapters, you'll find a myriad of tips and tricks. In fact, that's all the book is—a compilation of my favorite tips and tricks. In Chapter 1, for instance, you'll learn what programs are running in the background and how to disable them if they aren't needed, how to enable autologon, and how to configure specific programs to run when Windows boots. You'll also learn how to disable balloon tips, how to remove the Recycle Bin from the Desktop, how to remove your username from the Start menu, and more. All of this in Chapter 1! Tons of tips and tricks for hardcore users just like you.

As the book progresses, the tips and tricks become more advanced. In later chapters, you'll learn to configure Service Pack 2's firewall so that it's useful but functional, upgrade sound and video cards, use command-line tools such as `ping` and `ipconfig` to troubleshoot a network, create a local security policy, and configure account lockout and password policies for your users. The book contains hundreds of these kinds of tips and tricks—everything the hardcore user needs to know!

ELEMENTS YOU'LL RUN ACROSS WHILE READING AND BROWSING

All of us at Hardcore Central agreed early on that a book comprised solely of Windows XP tips and tricks would suit our hardcore audience better than any other format. We also wanted to make the book extremely user-friendly, so we also decided to add special elements and related icons throughout. Because of this format and the number of elements included, it may be of benefit to you to read through their descriptions before diving into the book.

The book comprises 11 chapters, each of which consists of a multitude of tips related to the chapter title. Each tip begins with a one-sentence description to give you a little more information beyond the tip title itself. Following this is a brief description of the subject matter, generally one to four paragraphs explaining the tip and the reasoning behind it. Lastly, step-by-step instructions detail how to carry out the procedure, almost always with an illustration or two to help you along the way.

Interspersed within the text are also several elements:

Notes provide ancillary info that's germane to a given discussion but not part of the main action.

Quick Tips give you information on best use of features, additional tidbits to make things easier, and time-saving shortcuts.

Watch Outs signal pitfalls to avoid, workarounds to employ, and "gotchas" to be aware of.

This element highlights cool utilities that are available for free online.

These tell you where to go for more information on a given topic or tip.

Now you're ready to go! Check out the Table of Contents and pick a tip that's of interest to you. Page on over to it and get ready to do some hardcore tweaking!

CHAPTER 1
THE USER INTERFACE

There are an incredible number of ways you can tweak your Windows XP computer for hardcore performance, so this first chapter starts with the most popular choices—speeding up the boot process and tweaking the user interface. Tweaking your computer using the tips and tricks in this chapter will benefit you in many ways: your machine will be faster, more responsive, and better suit your specific user needs. Tweaking isn't just for gamers and multimedia mavens anymore!

In this chapter you'll learn the top ways to get the most out of your computer, including disabling some items that start when your computer boots (decreasing how long this process takes and increasing computer performance), hiding the Welcome screen, disabling the Windows splash screen, getting rid of balloon tips, using TweakUI to take control of the user interface, and using the Group Policy Editor to disable the CTRL-ALT-DEL requirement on logon, just to name a few. The less your computer has to do, and the less you have to input, the better and faster you both will run!

THE NEED FOR SPEED

There are lots of things you can do that will help you enhance startup (or boot) performance. I'll introduce my favorite tricks and tips here.

Sweep Out the System Tray

The System Tray offers icons detailing what is running in the background while you work; removing as many as possible will increase performance.

The *System Tray*, more recently referred to by Microsoft as the *Notification Area*, is located on the right side of the Taskbar, the long rectangular box usually found at the bottom of your screen. The System Tray offers icons that detail what applications start automatically when Windows boots, and which are currently running in the background. Figure 1-1 shows a fairly

Notification Area (System Tray)

FIGURE 1-1 The Notification Area with running programs

busy System Tray, with multiple items active and running in the background in this order: new mail, a network connection, a printer, Full Shot (a screenshot capture application), an Internet connection, an antivirus program, MSN Messenger, another printer, and a pop-up stopper. These items are using valuable system resources. An arrow at the edge of the System Tray indicates that more items are in the System Tray; click it to see everything's that jammed in there. (The arrow appears because the Hide Inactive Icons option has been checked in the Taskbar and Start Menu Properties dialog box— more about these later in this chapter.)

Sometimes you can remove items from the System Tray by right-clicking them and choosing Exit, but others are a little more stubborn. In addition, removing the icons from the System Tray doesn't stop them from starting and putting their icons right back there the next time you boot up. If you want to remove items permanently, and prevent them from starting when Windows boots (making the bootup process noticeably faster and lightening the load on the CPU), perform the following steps:

1. Click Start | Run.

2. In the Run dialog box, type **msconfig.exe** and click OK.

3. In the System Configuration Utility dialog box, choose the Startup tab.

4. Uncheck any item you do not want to start up when Windows boots. Figure 1-2 shows some examples of what to uncheck. It's best to disable anything you've downloaded from the Internet but no longer want.

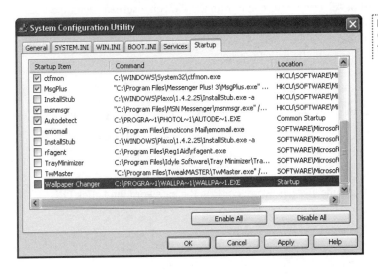

FIGURE 1-2 The System Configuration Utility's Startup tab and unnecessary programs

Only disable items you recognize. If you disable something that XP needs to run, such as RUNDLL32, you'll have problems, guaranteed!

5. You can increase the width of any category by dragging from its title bar. This will allow you to read each item's name more easily. Position the mouse in the Command title bar, for example, and when the arrow becomes a two-headed arrow, click and drag to the desired column length.
6. Click OK and then click Restart when prompted to reboot the computer. (Save your work and close all applications before you reboot.)
7. When your computer restarts, the System Configuration Utility dialog box will appear. Check the Don't Show This Message Or Launch The System Configuration Utility When Windows Starts option, and click OK.

This technique not only enhances startup performance, but can also be used to get rid of annoying pop-ups on bootup. Use the System Configuration Utility to disable registration programs, printer software that reminds you to buy more ink, and similar items.

Automate Everything You Can

Enable autologon to increase bootup performance.

If you are the only one who uses your computer and it's located in a secure area, there's no reason to continue wasting time entering your password or selecting your name from the Welcome screen each time you want to log on.

To enable autologon and bypass XP's prompt to enter a username and password, perform the following steps:

1. Click Start | Run.
2. In the Run dialog box, type **control userpasswords2** and click OK.
3. Uncheck Users Must Enter A User Name And Password To Use This Computer and click OK, as shown in Figure 1-3.
4. In the Automatically Log On dialog box that appears, type your username and password, confirm the password, and click OK.

FIGURE 1-3 Enable autologon

 You can also enable autologon using a PowerToy called TweakUI. PowerToys are free utilities you can download from the Internet that allow you to easily do things you would not normally be able to do (like add the Administrator account to the Welcome screen or enable autologon). There will be more on TweakUI later in this chapter.

↘ Prevent Windows Messenger from Starting Automatically

Windows Messenger starts automatically by default, but you can change this behavior.

Windows Messenger is the messaging utility that ships with Windows XP. By default, it starts automatically when you boot your computer. If you prefer MSN Messenger or another messaging program, or if you don't do any instant messaging, you'll want to stop Windows Messenger from booting.

The way in which you prevent Windows Messenger from starting automatically depends on whether you are using Outlook Express or Outlook.

In Outlook Express:

1. Click Tools | Options.

2. On the General tab, clear Automatically Log On To Windows Messenger. Click OK.

In Outlook:

1. Click Tools | Options.

2. On the Other tab, clear Enable Instant Messaging in Microsoft Outlook. Click OK.

The way in which you disable Windows Messenger from running altogether depends on which Windows operation system you are using. In Windows XP Professional:

1. Click Start | Run, and type **gpedit.msc**. Click OK.

2. Using the Group Policy Editor, under Local Computer Policy, expand Computer Configuration | Administrative Templates | Windows Components and select Windows Messenger, as shown in Figure 1-4.

FIGURE 1-4 The Group Policy Editor and Windows Messenger settings

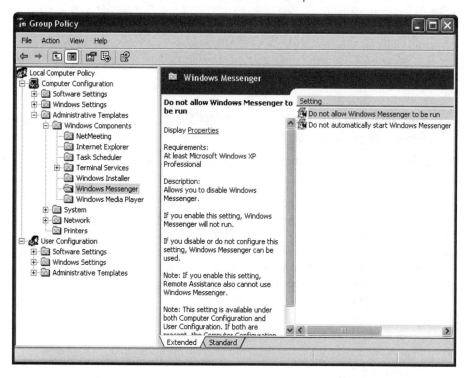

3. Double-click Do Not Allow Windows Messenger To Be Run, and select Enabled.
4. Click OK and close the Group Policy Editor.

In Windows XP Home:

1. Start Windows Messenger.
2. Click Tools | Options.
3. On the Preferences tab, clear Run This Program When Windows Starts. Click OK and reboot.

To completely rid your computer of Windows Messenger, visit ***http://www.support.microsoft.com*** *and search the Knowledge Base for article 302089.*

Allow a Specific Program to Start When the Computer Boots

If you use a specific program everyday, such as Outlook or Outlook Express, configure it to open automatically at bootup.

Now that you've killed what you don't need at bootup, you are ready to add some things you do need. If you always use a specific program when you start your computer, such as Outlook Express, Microsoft Word, or Adobe Photoshop, you can configure that program to open automatically each time you boot your computer. This won't speed up boot time, of course, but it will allow you to boot the computer and have the programs you always use open automatically.

To configure any program to start automatically when Windows boots:

1. Click Start | All Programs and point to the Startup folder. There may or may not be items in that folder. (Items in that folder *do* start automatically when Windows boots, so if there are unnecessary programs there you may want to remove them.)
2. On the All Programs menu, locate the program you want to have automatically start when you boot your computer.

3. Right-click that program and drag it to the Startup folder. If there are no items in the folder, drop it on top of Startup. If there are items in that folder, drag it over to the area where those items are listed and drop it there.

4. When you let go of the mouse, select Copy Here.

You can also browse to the Startup folder using Windows Explorer. Right-click Start and click Explore to open Windows Explorer. Under your local disk, expand Documents and Settings and find your user folder. Expand it, expand Start Menu, expand Programs, and select Startup. Figure 1-5 shows an example. Note that you can also drag items to this folder if you can't find them on the All Programs menu, including folders and files. Whatever you add here will open or start automatically on reboot.

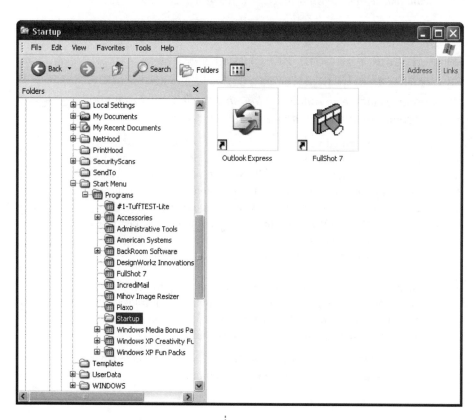

FIGURE 1-5 Windows Explorer and the Startup folder

↘ Allow the Administrator Account on the Welcome Screen

If you use the Administrator account only when you need to perform administrator tasks, enable the Administrator account on the Welcome screen.

Another way to enhance the bootup process is to enable the Administrator account on the Welcome screen. Enabling the Administrator account allows you to log on as an administrator when you need to, and to log on as a standard user or as a guest account when desirable.

Before enabling the Administrator account on the Welcome screen, you must meet certain criteria:

■ You must be part of a workgroup, not a domain.

■ You must be using the Welcome screen.

■ You must not be using Fast User Switching.

First, verify that the Welcome screen is enabled and that Fast User Switching is disabled by going to Start | Control Panel | User Accounts. In User Accounts:

1. Check Use The Welcome Screen. (If you don't see this option, you don't meet the criteria in the preceding bulleted list.)

2. Uncheck Use Fast User Switching.

Next, download, install, and configure TweakUI. TweakUI is a free PowerToy that lets you do almost anything to your user interface, and quite easily. One of the things you can do with TweakUI is show the Administrator account on the Welcome screen. Here's how:

1. Download TweakUI from **http://www.microsoft.com/windowsxp/ downloads/powertoys/xppowertoys.mspx**.

2. Open the program by clicking Start | All Programs | PowerToys For Windows XP | TweakUI For Windows XP.

3. Click Logon, and check Show "Administrator" On Welcome Screen, as shown in Figure 1-6.

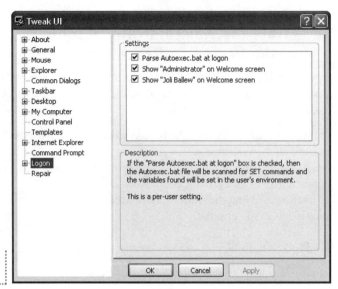

FIGURE 1-6 Using TweakUI to show the Administrator account

PERSONALIZE THE DESKTOP

Once your startup process is streamlined and you are logged on, you'll want to personalize the Desktop so that it fits you and your needs. As an author, I keep the Taskbar hidden and I stay away from screen savers but when I'm between projects I turn right back to using my own pictures as a background, locking the Taskbar, and customizing how my computer looks. Although most of these tasks are easy enough (and well known), other tweaks aren't. For instance, did you know you can put a toolbar on your Taskbar for the Desktop? Even with 15 open programs, files, and windows, you can reach anything on your Desktop in a single click. Let's look at that first.

 ## Tweak the Taskbar

The Taskbar is the doorway to all of the open programs on your computer; personalize it for the best performance possible.

Right-click an empty area of the Taskbar and point to Toolbars. Notice the options, including Desktop and Quick Launch. To add these or any others to the Taskbar, simply select them. While this is a simple enough task, what it offers up is quite useful. Take a look at the Taskbar in Figure 1-7.

FIGURE 1-7 Desktop toolbar on the Taskbar

From the Taskbar, you now can access everything on the Desktop. This is quite useful when multiple programs and files are open, and you need a specific item on the Desktop.

You can also tweak the Taskbar by right-clicking it and choosing Properties. From the Taskbar tab you can do the following:

- Lock the Taskbar

- Auto-hide the Taskbar

- Keep the Taskbar on top of other windows

- Group similar items on the Taskbar (or not)

- Show or hide Quick Launch

- Show or hide the clock

- Show or hide inactive icons

Set these to suit your needs. Personally, I couldn't do without the clock, and grouping similar items drives me crazy. However, I use the Quick Launch area every day, and find it most useful. (Quick Launch is the area to the left of the Taskbar just next to the Start menu. It holds icons for items you use regularly, and those items can be defined.)

 Want to add an item to the Quick Launch area? Locate it on the All Programs menu (or elsewhere), right-click the executable program icon, and drag it to the Quick Launch area of the Taskbar. Let go of the mouse and choose Copy Here. A new icon for the program will be added.

⬎ Use Your Own Picture as the Desktop Background

Put pictures on your Desktop so you can view them everyday.

While there are literally thousands of ways to personalize your computer, there's no better way to do so than with pictures. Pictures can be used as Desktop backgrounds (sometimes referred to as wallpaper) or as screen savers.

If you have a picture you'd like to use for the Desktop background:

1. Open the folder that contains the picture you want to use. If you've stayed organized and saved your pictures to the default folders, it should be in the My Pictures folder, which is usually in the My Documents folder.

2. Select the picture, but do not open it.

3. From the Picture Tasks pane, select Set As Desktop Background, as shown in Figure 1-8.

FIGURE 1-8 Use any image as Desktop wallpaper

If you prefer not to use the Picture Tasks pane, you can also right-click a picture and choose Set As Desktop Background from the menu that appears; this may be faster.

 *The Wallpaper Changer, a free PowerToy available from **http://www.microsoft.com/windowsxp/ downloads/powertoys/create_powertoys/default.mspx**, is a program that allows you to change the Desktop background automatically, at intervals you specify in minutes, hours, or even days. It's part of the PowerToys Fun Pack, a free, dependable, and fun set of applications.*

Create Your Own Screen Savers

Use your own pictures as a screen saver.

You can use your own pictures as screen savers too, by creating a slideshow of images in your picture library. Using the My Pictures Slideshow in the Control Panel's Display options, you can display images on the screen from anywhere between six seconds and three minutes before transitioning to the next image. Transitions vary, and range from fading in, to sliding in from a corner, to coming together in a checkerboard pattern.

 Back in the day, oh, the early '80s and into the '90s, screen savers were necessary to avoid an image "burning" into the screen. That's not believed to be true anymore, and screen savers are really just cosmetic.

To create a screen saver using your own images:

1. Open the My Pictures folder (or the folder where your images are stored) and verify that multiple pictures are saved in that folder.

2. Click Start | Control Panel. In Control Panel, open Display. You can also right-click an empty area of the Desktop and select Properties. (If you're in Category view, you'll have to pick Appearance and Themes first.)

 Control Panel has two views, Category and Classic. Classic view shows the icons without having to first choose a specific category. Category view requires that a category be selected first, as in Step 2.

3. Select the Screen Saver tab.

4. From the choices in the Screen Saver drop-down list, select My Pictures Slideshow.

5. Click Settings, and configure how often to change the picture, how much of the screen to use when displaying a picture, and what folder to use. Configure other settings as applicable. Click OK. You'll see a preview in the window, as shown in Figure 1-9.

FIGURE 1-9 Create a personalized screen saver

6. Click OK to close the Display Properties dialog box.

 *The Video Screen Saver PowerToy, a free PowerToy available from **http://www.microsoft.com/ windowsxp/downloads/powertoys/create_powertoys/default.mspx**, is a program that allows you to use your Windows Media Video files as your Windows XP screen saver. It's part of the PowerToys Fun Pack, a free, dependable, and fun set of applications.*

⬎ Disable the Windows Splash Screen

If you want to see the details of the bootup process, disable the splash screen.

Screen savers and backgrounds are one way to personalize your computer with pictures, but Windows XP has a few pictures of its own, one being the splash screen you see on bootup. There are multiple reasons why you'd want to disable the Windows splash screen. For starters, the splash screen hides the details regarding what files are being loaded as the computer boots, what version of XP you have, information about system data, information about the file system check, and more. When the splash screen covers that up, you don't get to see that part of the boot process. You may want to view this information for troubleshooting bootup problems, or perhaps just out of curiosity.

To disable the splash screen in Windows XP:

1. Right-click My Computer and choose Properties.

2. Click the Advanced tab, and click the Settings button under Startup and Recovery.

3. In the System Startup area, click Edit.

4. After the /fastdetect entry under [operating systems], add a space and /SOS. It should look something like this, although systems vary:

```
[boot loader]
timeout=3
default=multi(0)disk(0)rdisk(0)partition(1)\WINDOWS
[operating systems]
multi(0)disk(0)rdisk(0)partition(1)\WINDOWS=
 "Microsoft Windows XP Professional" /fastdetect /
 SOS
```

5. Click File | Save. Click OK to apply and close the System Properties dialog box.

6. Restart the computer and the splash screen will be gone.

PLAY MASTER AND COMMANDER
WITH TweakUI

TweakUI is a free PowerToy that lets you do all kinds of cool things with Windows XP, things you probably didn't think you could do without having the nerves of steel it takes to edit the Registry. Among other things, TweakUI lets you enable or disable ToolTip animations and fades, as well as (those annoying) balloon tips, and offers easy access to the Group Policy Editor, where you can change the most intricate aspects of the computer's behavior.

 *You can download TweakUI from **http://www.microsoft.com/windowsxp/downloads/ powertoys/xppowertoys.mspx**. You open the program by clicking Start | All Programs | PowerToys For Windows XP | TweakUI For Windows XP.*

The TweakUI interface is easy to use and is shown in Figure 1-10. To configure any setting, click and/or expand any category, browse through the options, and make changes as desired. The program does all the work and automatically applies the changes. Although there are literally hundreds of options available, the following sections introduce my favorites. (You can perform many of these tasks on your own and without TweakUI, but TweakUI does make it easier.)

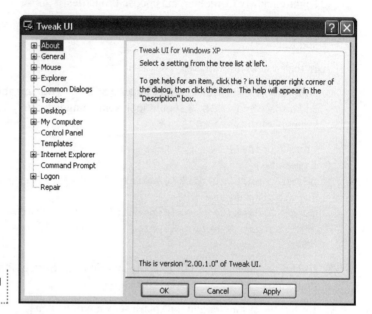

FIGURE 1-10 The TweakUI interface

◥ Personalize the Start Menu

You don't have to settle for the generic Start menu and its choices; personalize it to make it your own.

You can right-click the Start button, choose Properties, and configure settings for Windows XP's Start menu. For instance, you can choose to use XP's Start menu interface, or opt for the Classic Start menu used in earlier versions of the operating system. From either menu, you can set how to display Start menu items, including displaying (or not displaying) the following (among others):

- Control Panel
- Help and Support

- My Computer

- My Documents

- My Music

Once you choose which elements you're going to display, you then specify whether additional options should be shown as a link or as a menu. One thing you can't set, though, is what can and can't be shown in the Frequently Used Programs list. Figure 1-11 shows this list as it appears on my computer.

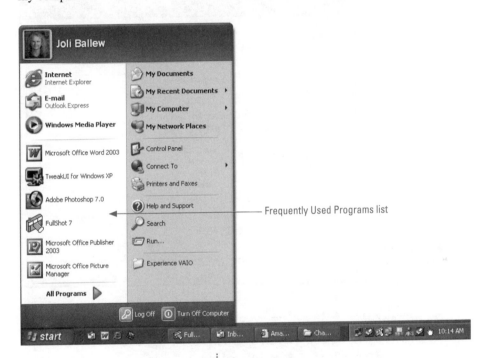

FIGURE 1-11 Frequently Used Programs list on the Start menu

To decide what items make the cut and appear on this list, Windows XP keeps track of how often you open and use any program. As you use programs, the program name gets moved up the list. With a new XP installation, the first program you open gets placed there. As you use others more and more, they move up the ladder so to speak, and are placed on this list above the others, and eventually unpopular programs are moved off. To tell Windows XP what programs you *never* want to see on the list (perhaps you play

FreeCell or use Windows Media Player at work every day, but don't want either to appear):

1. Open TweakUI.

2. Expand Taskbar.

3. Select XP Start Menu.

4. Deselect any items you never want to appear, as shown in Figure 1-12.

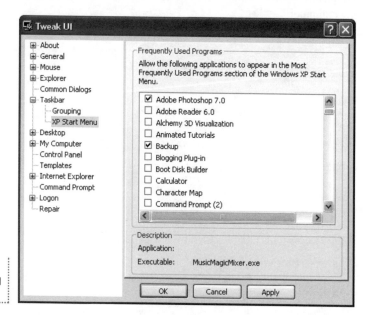

FIGURE 1-12 Disallow certain items from the Frequently Used Programs list

↘ Configure Image Quality and Size of Thumbnails in Windows Explorer

TweakUI offers an easy way to set image quality and thumbnail size.

You can tweak the size and quality of the thumbnails you see in the My Pictures, My Documents, and similar folders. Image quality can be lessened for better performance, as can size. Larger thumbnails require more memory and disk space. Both settings are per-user settings, meaning they change when a different user logs on.

To use TweakUI to configure image quality for thumbnails in Windows Explorer:

1. Open TweakUI and expand Explorer.

2. Click Thumbnails.

3. For a higher-quality thumbnail, move the Image Quality slider to the right.

4. To change the size of the thumbnails, select a new size in the Thumbnail, Size (Pixels) option.

A larger thumbnail is useful in certain circumstances—a person with poor eyesight or one who sits far away from the monitor, for instance. A high-quality thumbnail may also be important to an artist or photographer. But keep in mind that larger images require the computer to work harder. Since big images require more memory and disk space, they should only be used if absolutely necessary. The largest and highest-quality settings will offer a noticeable performance hit when opening the Explorer folder. On the other hand, smaller sizes and quality use less resources, and may be beneficial to those with limited reserves. Figure 1-13 shows the My Pictures folder configured to show thumbnails of images at 250 pixels, and the highest quality on the slider.

FIGURE 1-13 Thumbnails can be changed in size and quality.

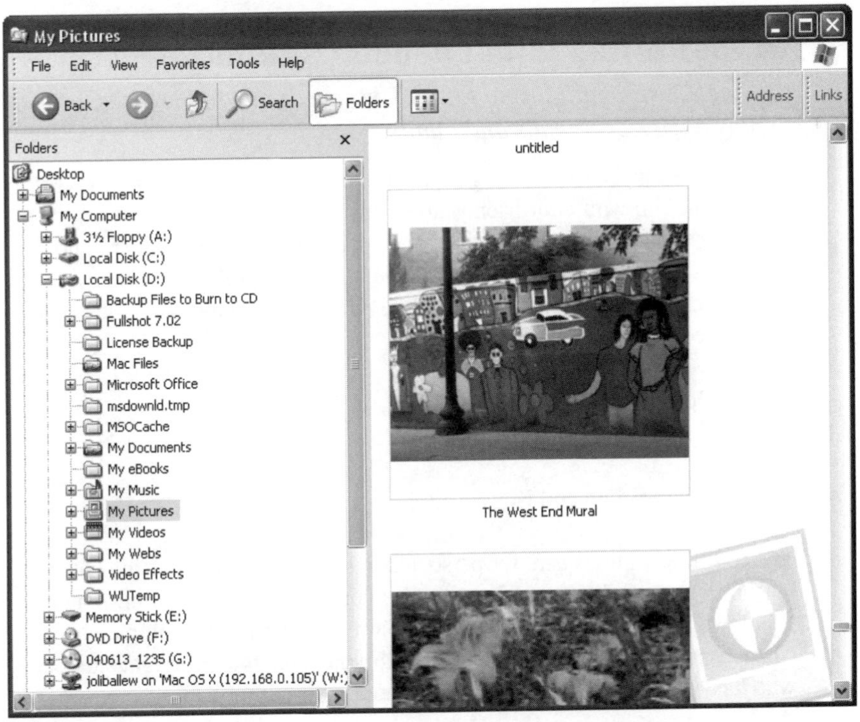

↘ Pop Those Balloon Tips

Balloon tips are those annoying little pop-ups from XP; get rid of them with TweakUI.

This is a pretty easy one, but you can amaze your friends and family by easily disabling (turning off) those annoying pop-up balloon tips that appear in the right corner of the Taskbar. These balloon tips tell you various things—you should take a tour of XP, get a .NET passport, etc.—and after a month or two they can get pretty annoying.

To disable balloon tips:

1. Open TweakUI.

2. Click the Taskbar option.

3. Clear the Disable Balloon Tips check box.

 If you want to see just how many balloon tips appear for a new user of Windows XP or for a clean installation, log on as an administrator, open Control Panel and User Accounts, create a new user, and then log on as that user. You'll see why TweakUI's Disable Balloon Tips option is necessary.

↘ Set a Trap with Changed Settings

Change the keyboard layout to suit your needs and preferences, or just to play a trick on friends and family.

Perhaps this doesn't belong here, or even in this book, but if you want to have a little fun with your friends and family, especially those that use your computer without your permission, consider changing the keyboard and mouse setup to something only you understand and prefer. Here's how.

If your keyboard comes with command keys, like Favorites, Cut, Copy, Paste, Media, or other options:

1. Open TweakUI.

2. Expand Explorer.

3. Select Command Keys.

You'll see options here for personalizing those keys. Change the Favorites button to open Solitaire, change the Lower Microphone button to open Windows Media Player, or use Mute Volume to turn up the volume instead. Chances are these little changes will help you catch that midnight snooper who has been using your computer without your authorization!

You can also change the mouse settings. Just click Mouse and make any changes desired. You can change the mouse click sensitivity settings, drag settings, hover settings, and more. You can make it difficult for almost anyone to use the mouse at all! (On a more practical side, though, you can configure mouse settings for those that have a hard time using a mouse, such as a person with arthritis or a disability.)

USE THE GROUP POLICY EDITOR TO TAKE CONTROL OF XP

Now that you've had a little fun, let's look at some settings that can be configured that are bit more practical. The Group Policy Editor offers literally thousands of setting combinations that allow an administrator to define a user's or group of users' Desktop environment. This includes how the Desktop looks to users, such as whether or not they can access specific icons or perform specific tasks like changing the Desktop background.

Group policies are set for two reasons: to secure a *computer* by configuring Computer Configuration settings, and to limit what *users* can do while at the computer, which is configured through User Configuration settings. Although group policies are generally created by administrators of networks for large groups of users for the purpose of securing a work environment, you can configure the settings in the Group Policy Editor to personalize your own environment at your local computer.

 You can open the Group Policy Editor easily from inside TweakUI. Expand About, and select Policy.

↘ Be in Command of the Control Panel

Remove applets, hide items, hide specific tabs, and otherwise make the Control Panel off limits to users.

You can take control of the Control Panel by using the Group Policy Editor. You can prohibit access to the Control Panel, hide or show only certain Control Panel applets, and even force the Classic Control Panel style. Drilling down deeper into the options, you can completely personalize the Display Properties dialog box by hiding specific items, such as the Desktop tab, the Appearance and Themes tab, the Screen Saver tab, and more. This is only the beginning. You'll want to take some time to browse through all of the options before deciding what (if anything) you want to configure.

To see what is available and to make changes to the Control Panel:

1. Open the Group Policy Editor and expand User Configuration | Administrative Templates, and then click Control Panel. The Control Panel options will appear in the right pane.

2. To enable any option, double-click it and choose Enable. To disable any option, double-click it and choose Disable.

3. Under the Control Panel options in the Group Policy Editor, select Display.

4. Double-click Remove Display From Control Panel and, in the resulting dialog box, choose Enabled. Click OK.

5. Open the Control Panel and then open Display. You'll get the message box shown in Figure 1-14.

6. After browsing through the options, make sure to undo these actions, unless you want to keep them.

FIGURE 1-14 Disabling Display properties

7. Close the Group Policy Editor.

 Turn Off Personalized Menus

Personalized menus only show you what you use most often, and you can turn this off.

The previous section was rather generic, with an introduction to the Group Policy Editor, some brief information on how to use it, and a view of just how much can be achieved with it. Now, you'll move on to more specific tasks, such as turning off (what some of us believe to be) those annoying personalized menus.

Personalized menus, those menus in Internet Explorer's Favorites menu, Word's File and Edit menus, and similar places, only show what you use most often, and don't show you the rest of the items available unless you wait a second or two or click the arrow at the bottom of the menu itself. Some people find this rather bothersome, and would like to turn this feature off.

Although there is more than one way to do that, here's one way using the Group Policy Editor (while you're here, check out all the other settings):

1. Using the Group Policy Editor, expand User Configuration | Administrative Templates | Windows Components and select Start Menu And Taskbar.

2. About halfway down the right pane, double-click Turn Off Personalized Menus.

3. From the resulting dialog box, choose Enable to turn off personalized menus.

Notice in this same pane that you can remove the user's name from the Start menu, hide the Notification Area, remove Logoff from the Start menu, and more.

Clear My Recent Documents List on Exit

You don't have to keep an open and updated list of recent documents if you don't want to.

As with other Start menu options, right-clicking the Start button and selecting Properties allows you to configure the My Recent Documents item that appears on the Start menu. You can choose to show all your recent documents or show none at all, or to manually clear the list yourself. If you want the list to be cleared automatically when you log off, you have to open the Group Policy Editor, locate the appropriate setting, and enable the option to clear the My Recent Documents history on exit. Here's how:

1. Click Start | Run and type **gpedit.msc**. Click OK.

2. Under Local Computer Policy, expand User Configuration | Administrative Templates and select Start Menu And Taskbar.

3. Scroll down about halfway through the list and double-click Clear History Of Recently Opened Documents On Exit.

4. Select Enabled, and click OK.

You can also turn off the My Recent Documents feature permanently, which may be a better solution. If you prefer not to use the Group Policy Editor, just right-click Start, choose Properties | Customized | Advanced, and uncheck List My Most Recently Opened Documents.

Disable the CTRL-ALT-DEL Requirement

CTRL-ALT-DEL may not be necessary in your private and secure environment.

The previous Group Policy configuration changes have been located in the User Configuration area of the Group Policy Editor. Let's look now at some computer-related items, specifically, disabling the requirement to use CTRL-ALT-DEL to log on to the computer, the so-called "three-finger salute" that is the bane of computer users everywhere. If you are the only one using the computer and it's in a safe place, there's no reason to continue to take this step when logging on; it will only slow you down.

To stop requiring CTRL-ALT-DEL during logon (you'll still be able to use it inside Windows XP to get to Task Manager):

1. In the Group Policy Editor, expand Computer Configuration | Windows Settings | Security Settings | Local Policies and select Security Options.
2. Double-click Interactive Logon: Do Not Require CTRL+ALT+DEL.
3. From the resulting dialog box, select Enabled, and click OK.

Notice also from this pane that you can disable the Guest account (which may be a wise choice if you aren't expecting guests, since no password is required by default), stop displaying the last logged-on user's name if multiple users log on, and configure a text message that each user will see when logging on. I suggest that you avoid changing system settings such as the type of sharing and security model used for local accounts or anything similar; otherwise, you may find yourself in a mess the next time you need to troubleshoot a problem with your computer.

If you make a change you think you may not remember, or one that might negatively impact the performance of your computer, write down what change you make in case you have to go back and reverse it.

Remove Unwanted Icons from the Desktop

Keep your Desktop free of clutter by removing what you don't use.

The Desktop has lots of icons on it by default, including the Recycle Bin, My Documents, Internet Explorer, and others. While many people enjoy having these icons at their fingertips, others would rather have a nice, clean Desktop with nothing on it at all, or at least a minimal amount of icons. TweakUI again makes this task quite simple.

To remove the Recycle Bin from the Desktop using TweakUI:

1. Open TweakUI.

2. Click Desktop.

3. Uncheck Recycle Bin.

You can also remove the Recycle Bin by using the Group Policy Editor. The Group Policy Editor offers more than TweakUI, though; for instance, you can also remove the Desktop Cleanup Wizard, prohibit adjustment of the Desktop toolbars, and more. As with previous tips, these options are located in the Group Policy Editor by expanding User Configuration | Administrative Templates and selecting the appropriate item, in this case Desktop. These choices are shown in Figure 1-15.

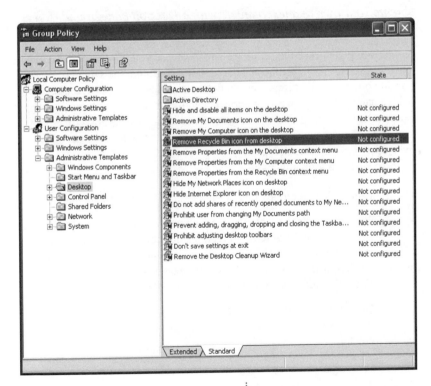

FIGURE 1-15 Desktop choices in the Group Policy Editor

THEMES: TO ENHANCE, OR NOT TO ENHANCE

Up to now, I've been talking mostly about enhancing the computer's performance, but now I'll move to enhancing how it looks, with themes. Themes offer a great way to spice up your desktop and computer interface, but be aware that this new look comes with a price. Themes are RAM-hogging, performance-depleting, CPU-using, but *extremely* cool software tools that allow you to personalize your computer using sounds, colors, fonts, Desktop background pictures, screen savers, and even mouse pointers.

To see what themes you have available on your own computer, open Control Panel (available from the Start menu), open Display, and click the Themes tab. You may only have a couple—the Windows XP theme and the Windows Classic theme—but you can get more or create your own.

 Create Your Own Theme

Create your own theme, complete with a Desktop background, screen saver, and other personalizations.

Creating your own theme allows you to choose your Desktop background, choose a screen saver, set the appearance, and configure the screen resolution to suit your personal preferences, and then save those changes as a theme with a name you'll recognize. People generally create different themes for specific tasks, such as book writing, music making, or working with digital images. You may create several themes yourself, and switch between them when performing those tasks.

To create your own theme:

1. Right-click an empty area of the Desktop and choose Properties.

2. Configure a desktop background, choose a screen saver, set the appearance, configure the screen resolution, and make whatever other changes you deem necessary. There are many, many settings. Take your time to visit each tab, and make changes as you desire. What I've mentioned here is in no way all of the options.

3. Once the settings are configured the way you want them, from the Themes tab, select Save As, and save them under a name you create.

⤷ Where to Find Themes

Locate themes online, at stores, and hidden inside other software.

You can purchase software packages that contain themes, such as Microsoft Plus! or the Microsoft Plus! SuperPack, which includes Plus! Aquarium, Plus! Space, Plus! Nature, and Plus! daVinci. Plus! Nature is shown in Figure 1-16. Although you may not be able to see everything here, the Desktop is a raindrop on a tree, the mouse pointer is a leaf, and the colors are brown and green. The system sounds are changed as well, and a mouse click sounds like a cricket chirping.

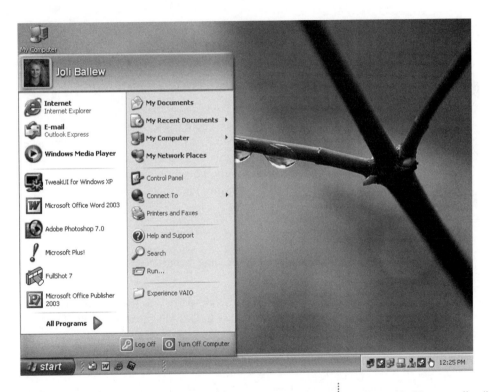

FIGURE 1-16 Themes offer diversity.

You can also download themes from the Internet. Some are free; some you have to purchase. Here are some of my favorite places to find themes online:

- **http://www.themexp.org**   Not only does ThemeXP.org offer lots of free themes, but you can also create your own and submit them.

- **http://themes.belchfire.net**   This site, Belchfire.net, offers lots of free themes, but lots of pop-up ads too. Once you get past the pop-ups, though, you'll find all kinds of customizable, free, goodies.

- **http://windows-xp-themes.com**   This is a nice site and offers what is referred to there as a *skin*, which changes the whole look of Windows XP.

 *For more information about working with themes, read the Windows XP Expert Zone article by Jerry Moskowitz located at **http://www.microsoft.com/windowsxp/using/setup/expert/ moskowitz_03february17.mspx**.*

↘ Technical Considerations when Using Themes

Use themes only if you're willing to give up a little performance too.

As mentioned earlier, although themes may look nice and offer sounds and screens you've never heard or seen before, they will slow down your computer. It doesn't matter how much RAM or what kind of CPU you have either; running a theme in the background at all times simply causes the computer to have to work harder every moment it's turned on.

Here are some of the problems you can expect if you use themes:

- You'll often find that while trying to wake the computer from hibernation or sleep, it will hang.

- The mouse pointers used in some themes make it difficult to click where you need to click.

- Themes you download from third-party web sites can consist of poorly written code and cause hard-to-diagnose problems. They may also contain viruses.

- The computer runs slowly and is not responsive.

I mention this only because I think *hard core* means fast and lean, but you may think *hard core* means the computer looks and feels personalized for your specific wants and needs. If that's what you want, go for it. Just be prepared to wait a little longer for windows and files to open!

Moving forward from the visual aspects of XP, in the next chapter you'll learn about applications and services that can slow the computer down, or help you out of a jam.

CHAPTER 2
WINDOWS XP APPLICATIONS AND SERVICES

Windows XP comes with many full-blown applications that you've probably used, such as Microsoft Paint and Windows Movie Maker, but it also comes with lesser-known applications that walk you through specific tasks, like installing or running a program that was created for another Windows operating system. That application is called the Program Compatibility Wizard, and I'll discuss that in this chapter. There are other applications that I will discuss throughout the book, including Remote Assistance, which allows you to get assistance from an online buddy; Remote Desktop, which allows you to connect to your office and work from home; System Restore, which allows you to revert to an earlier date to repair a computer problem; and Disk Cleanup, which allows you to delete unnecessary files, just to name a few.

Windows XP also ships with numerous services. A service is a type of application too, but services run constantly in the background. Services you may be familiar with are Fast User Switching Compatibility, Plug and Play, Print Spooler, and Windows Time. Each service is always ready when you need it.

You may or may not need all of the available applications and services, and you can stop unnecessary services to provide better computer performance. Remember, as mentioned in Chapter 1, the less your computer has to do in the background, the more resources it will have available when you need to run resource-intensive programs or multiple applications simultaneously. In this chapter, you'll learn which services are not always necessary and how to disable them.

USING WIZARDS

One of my favorite Windows XP applications is the Program Compatibility Wizard. This wizard allows you to run older programs or games that were not created for Windows XP. Although you'll ultimately want to upgrade all of your applications to ones that are compatible, sometimes this isn't an option. As an example, you may have used a résumé program with Windows 98 that no longer runs on your Windows XP machine. To edit your saved résumés in Windows XP, you would most likely have to install the program, because most older applications such as this save in proprietary file formats that aren't editable in other programs. As another example, you may need to open and edit files created in a graphics program that is currently incompatible with Windows XP. Perhaps the company that created the program went out of business or discontinued the software. If you've run into these or similar problems, you can use the Program Compatibility Wizard and install and run the older program anyway. It's as simple as working through the wizard, which is shown in Figure 2-1.

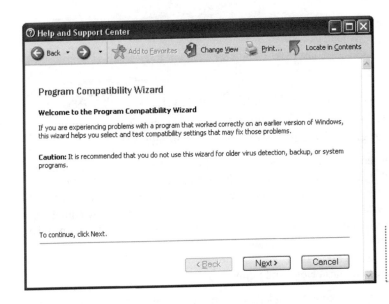

FIGURE 2-1 The Program Compatibility Wizard can be opened from the Help and Support Center.

 The Program Compatibility Wizard offers several ways to configure older programs so that they'll run properly on Windows XP.

There are several ways to increase how well a program functions in various modes, and the Program Compatibility Wizard offers some choices when configuring the options. You'll learn how to configure the wizard so that you can do the following:

■ Choose an operating system, including Windows 95, Windows NT 4.0 (SP5), Windows 98, Windows Me, and Windows 2000.

■ Select display settings, including 256 colors, 640×480 screen resolution, or disabling themes altogether.

■ Choose the option to install or start the program, test it, and then return to the wizard if the program still does not work as expected.

The best choice for the first option is the operating system the program was originally created for. In the case of the résumé program mentioned earlier, you would choose Windows 98. Even if a program runs on a later OS, still select the OS the program was created for. The best choice for the second option is the recommended setting suggested by the manufacturer of the program. This option is included because many older games will only function under specific resolutions, like 640×480, and selecting this option is sometimes the only choice that needs to be made.

For best results, Microsoft suggests you don't use the Program Compatibility Wizard to run programs such as antivirus or backup utilities.

➘ Using the Program Compatibility Wizard

Use the Program Compatibility Wizard when you need to run an older program that was not created for Windows XP.

I haven't found a more reliable way to open the Program Compatibility Wizard than by browsing through the Help and Support Center. On some computers, the Program Compatibility Wizard can be located by clicking Start | All Programs | Accessories, although it isn't located there on my computer. It is on a friend's computer, though, so to be safe, I suggest that you open the Program Compatibility Wizard this way:

1. Click Start | Help And Support.

2. Select Fixing A Problem, near the bottom of the left column. From the resulting Fixing A Problem list, select Application And Software Problems, which is shown in Figure 2-2.

FIGURE 2-2   Locate the Program Compatibility Wizard

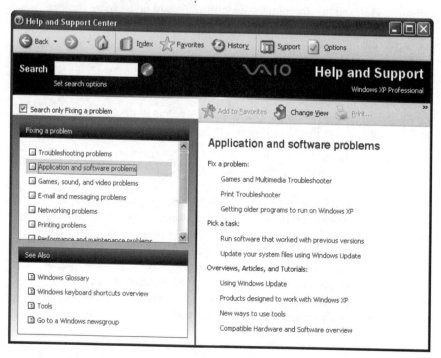

3. From the results, click Getting Older Programs To Run On Windows XP.

4. In the article that appears, locate and click Start The Program Compatibility Wizard. Click Next to start the wizard.

You then have options for locating the program, as shown in Figure 2-3.

FIGURE 2-3 The three options for locating the program to configure settings

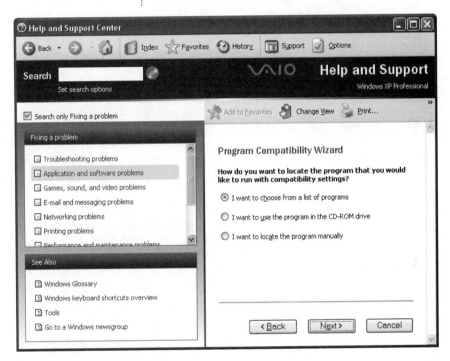

5. If the CD is in the CD-ROM drive, select I Want To Use The Program In The CD-ROM Drive and click Next. If the CD is not available and the program is stored on the hard drive or on a network, select I Want To Locate The Program Manually, and then click Next.

6. If you chose to install from a CD, skip this step. If searching manually for an application, click Browse. Locate and select the application's installation or setup file. Sometimes this is called setup.exe, or it is the name of the program itself. Generally, there's an icon for this file in the Programs folder on the C: drive. If you have trouble manually locating the program folder on the hard drive, in the Look In window select Local Disk (generally C:), expand Documents And Settings, expand the folder that contains your username, expand Start Menu, and expand Programs. The program's folder will probably be in there.

To configure settings for a program that's already installed, select I Want To Choose From A List Of Programs, then click Next. A list of programs appears. Once you select the program you're looking for:

1. Continue with the wizard by selecting the original operating system the program was created for. Click Next.

2. Select the display settings suggested by the program manufacturer, generally noted on the packaging. Click Next.

3. To test the new settings, click Next. If the program runs as it should, close the program, and select Yes, Set This Program To Always Use These Compatibility Settings. If the result was not satisfactory, select No, Try Different Compatibility Settings.

FIGURE 2-4 Configure program compatibility settings

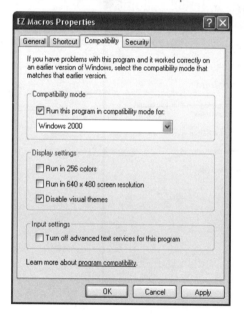

You can also set compatibility settings by right-clicking any installed program and selecting Properties. Every program's Properties dialog box has a Compatibility tab, but not all programs offer the ability to change these settings. For instance, right-clicking Windows Media Player 10, a program created by Microsoft specifically for Windows XP, has all of the compatibility options grayed out and unavailable. Conversely, many third-party programs' Compatibility options are available, as shown in Figure 2-4.

STOP UNWANTED XP SERVICES

Now that you have all of the older programs you want to run working properly with Windows XP, it's time to take a look at some things that run in the background, likely without your knowledge. These are called services, and they are programs too. Unwanted or unnecessary services can be stopped, started, paused, or resumed by the administrator of the computer (a person with administrator rights). Services can also be configured to run automatically or manually, or they can be completely disabled. If you have Windows XP Professional, you can view all services from the Services console, which you open by clicking Start | All Programs | Administrative Tools | Services. If you have Windows XP Home, you'll have to click Start | Search, type in Administrative Tools, click Search, and open the folder from there. (In Windows XP Home, Administrative Tools are not listed on the All Programs list.) The Services window is shown in Figure 2-5.

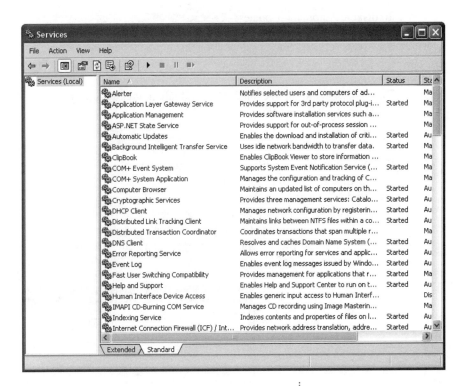

FIGURE 2-5 Services in the Services console

Not all of these services are necessary, and you can disable several of them, but you shouldn't just go randomly mucking about disabling a service because you don't like its name or don't believe it's really needed. Most services are needed. However, there are a few you can disable, and in doing so, you can decrease the load the computer must bear just to run.

➘ Disable Automatic Updates

Disable or stop Automatic Updates to increase resources for high-performance tasks.

Automatic Updates are Windows XP's way of keeping your computer up-to-date, in the background, by automatically checking for, downloading, and even installing updates that Microsoft releases. It's best to leave this setting on Automatic, but if you want to increase performance for a computer used for gaming or other high-performance needs, you can disable (or stop) Automatic Updates.

To disable Automatic Updates:

1. In the Services console, double-click Automatic Updates.

2. To stop the service temporarily, on the General tab, click Stop.

3. To disable the service, on the General tab, in the Startup Type options, click Disable.

4. Click OK.

If you have multiple profiles created, for instance a gaming profile (as detailed in Chapter 6), you can disable services for that specific profile only. If you do use your computer for gaming, you'll probably want to disable as many services as possible for the best performance possible. To disable a service for a specific hardware profile, click the Log On tab in Step 3, select the profile to apply the change to, and click Disable. This option is shown in Figure 2-6.

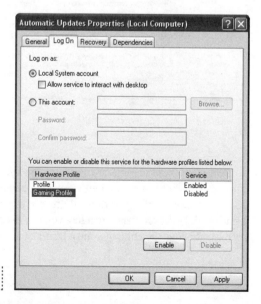

FIGURE 2-6 Disabling a service for a single profile

2

➘ Stop the Error Reporting Service

If you are tired of reporting errors to Microsoft or being prompted to, turn that service off.

When an application error occurs with your computer, Windows XP tries to send an error report to Microsoft; it asks for your permission with an annoying little pop-up box that you've probably seen. You can disable or stop this service to prevent the box from appearing, and to stop the reporting of errors. If you're into your privacy, or just want a little peace and quiet, disable or stop the Error Reporting Service:

1. From the Services console, double-click Error Reporting Service. (Remember, in Windows XP Home, the Services console can be opened by clicking Start | Search and searching for and opening the Administrative Tools folder, in which you click Services. In Windows XP Professional, you can open Administrative Tools from the All Programs list.)

2. To stop the service, on the General tab, click Stop.

3. To disable the service, on the General tab, in the Startup Type options, click Disable.

4. Click Apply, and then click OK.

➘ Disable Fast User Switching

Increase performance by disabling or not using Fast User Switching.

Fast User Switching lets users switch between user accounts without having to log off. While this is convenient, the computer has to keep up with each logged-on user's programs, e-mail, and open files. This creates quite a drain on system resources. Consider how much work a computer would have to do to run Photoshop CS for one logged-on user, and Movie Maker 2 and Outlook Express for another. It's a lot to keep up with.

If you don't want to use this option, you can disable it. To disable or stop Fast User Switching:

1. In the Services console, double-click Fast User Switching Compatibility.

2. To stop the service, on the General tab, click Stop.

3. To disable the service, on the General tab, in the Startup Type options, click Disable.

4. Click Apply, and then click OK.

↘ Stop the Indexing Service

The Indexing Service is a major resource-using hog; it's best to disable it.

The Indexing Service indexes the contents and properties of files on the local computer (and on remote ones if so configured). The indexing is done regularly, kicks in seemingly whenever it wants to, and causes the computer to slow down and perform poorly. This usually happens just at the same moment you're playing a game or rendering a movie, or at least it seems to. The art of indexing uses massive amounts of RAM and CPU resources, and in my opinion, isn't worth it for what it offers.

So what does it offer? Well, the Indexing Service allows you to locate specific files by querying the database using a specific query language. I'll introduce that service and language later in this chapter in "Use the Indexing Service." Using this service, you can search for files on the computer using something as miniscule as a specific word the file contains, among other things. Again, though, the costs far outweigh the benefits.

Disabling the Indexing Service does not disable or affect the regular Search options.

If you do decide to rid the computer of this service (and you might want to wait until after you read more about it later in this chapter), you'll first want to uninstall it by using the Add/Remove applet via Control Panel:

1. Click Start | Control Panel.

2. Click Add Or Remove Programs.

3. Click Add/Remove Windows Components and wait while the list is populated.

4. A new window will appear named Windows Components Wizard. In this dialog box, in the Windows Components list, uncheck Indexing Service and click Next.

5. Click Finish when complete. Figure 2-7 shows the de-installation in progress.

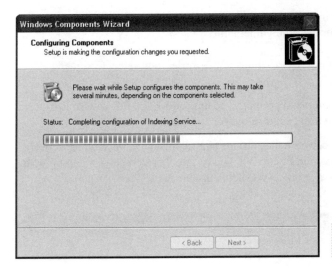

FIGURE 2-7 Uninstall the Indexing Service

2

Once the Indexing Service is uninstalled, you are ready to disable it:

1. Open the Services console as detailed earlier.

2. Double-click the Indexing Service.

3. On the General tab, in the Startup Type options, click Disable.

4. Click OK.

↘ Disable Messenger

Most home users don't need the Messenger service and thus may disable it.

The Messenger service is not related to Windows Messenger. The Messenger service is related to the net send command and Alerter service messages sent between clients and servers. This service was originally created for system administrators to notify their Windows network clients about network activity, such as shutting down the network for maintenance, and to make company-wide announcements. Recently, advertisers have learned how to open pop-up windows on your computer using this service, and this produces unwanted spam and potential access to viruses. Because of these things, it's actually in the best interest of most home users to disable this service.

To find out if you can receive net send messages, test your computer configuration for net send vulnerability:

1. Click Start | All Programs | Accessories, and select Command Prompt.

2. At the command prompt, type **net send 127.0.0.1 You've just received a net send message**.

3. If you receive a notice that the alias could not be found on the network, as is shown in Figure 2-8, you're safe. If you receive a pop-up with this message on it, you should disable the service.

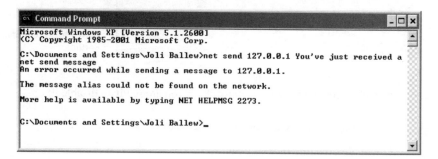

FIGURE 2-8 Testing for net send vulnerability

⬊ Disable Themes

Check out what your computer would look like if you didn't use themes.

If you just want a plain-vanilla usable and high-performance computer, and you don't care about using the new XP theme or any other, you can disable the Themes service. Themes use RAM, perhaps as much as 12MB. That's a respectable amount, especially if you only have 256MB. To preview what your computer would look like with Themes disabled, stop the service first before you decide to disable it. You'll be able to tell immediately if you like the new look or not. If you don't, simply restart the service:

1. Open the Services console as detailed earlier. (By now, it's probably in the Frequently Used Programs area of the Start menu.)

2. Double-click Themes.

3. Click Stop to see what happens. Open a few windows, programs, and applications to get the full effect.

4. To disable the service, in the Startup Type options, click Disable.

5. Click OK.

REMOVE RECOGNITION SERVICES

Windows XP comes with two recognition services, Handwriting Recognition and Speech Recognition. If you don't use them, you should remove them. Both use computer memory and can cause a noticeable effect on computer performance. Removing handwriting and speech recognition services does not remove them from your computer, though, it only prevents them from loading into memory. If you decide you need them later, you can enable them.

⬎ Remove Handwriting Recognition

Handwriting Recognition should be removed if it isn't being used.

Handwriting Recognition is a text service that ships with Windows XP that allows you to use an input device, such as a digital pen and tablet, to enter text by writing it on the tablet rather than typing it in. Other devices include mouse pads you can write on or tablet PCs. If you aren't using any handwriting devices, you should remove this option.

To remove Handwriting Recognition:

1. Click Start | Control Panel | Regional And Language Options. (If you're in Category view, you'll need to select Date, Time, Language, And Regional Options first.)

2. On the Languages tab, under Text Services And Input Languages, click Details. Clicking Details opens the Text Services And Input Languages dialog box.

3. Under Installed Services, select Handwriting Recognition for each language for which it is not needed (you may only have one language configured), and click Remove (see Figure 2-9). (If you don't have any option to remove Handwriting Recognition, you never installed it.)

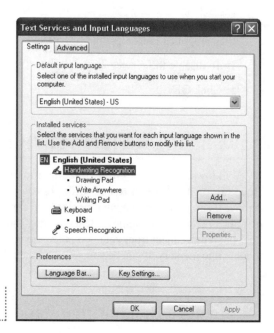

FIGURE 2-9 Remove Handwriting Recognition services

↘ Remove Speech Recognition

Speech Recognition should be removed if it isn't being used.

Speech Recognition is a text service that ships with Windows XP that allows you to use a input device, such as a microphone, to speak text rather than type it in. As with Handwriting Recognition, if you aren't using any handwriting devices, you should remove this option, since it requires computer memory and other resources and may affect performance.

To remove Speech Recognition:

1. Click Start | Control Panel | Regional And Language Options. (If you're in Category view, you'll need to select Date, Time, Language, And Regional Options first.)

2. On the Languages tab, under Text Services And Input Languages, click Details.

3. Under Installed Services, select Speech Recognition for each language for which it is not needed (you may only have one language configured), and click Remove.

USE THE INDEXING SERVICE

The Indexing Service is another service that ships with Windows XP that is likely not needed. The Indexing Service indexes documents by their properties and stores the information in a catalog, a type of database. Once your documents are indexed, you can use the Indexing Service to search those documents using their specific attributes. Searching can be done from the Search option or through your web browser.

While this service can be quite helpful and convenient for those who need it, it won't offer much to the average home user, and will instead slow down the performance of the computer when it gets on its indexing jag. However, if you feel this service will benefit you or your business, by all means give it a shot.

 Earlier in this chapter, in "Stop Unwanted XP Services," I suggested removing and then disabling the Indexing Service. However, I also suggested that you wait until after you've read this section, just in case it looks like something you'd be interested in. If you already uninstalled the service, it can be just as easily reinstalled using the Add Or Remove Programs applet in Control Panel.

◥ Track Down the Indexing Service

Check to see if the Indexing Service is running on your computer.

The Indexing Service is available from the Computer Management console, and you can use this console to configure, control, and query the service. As mentioned earlier, the Indexing Service is not necessary for the average home user, and may be running in the background unnecessarily, using system resources.

To open this console and access the service to see if it's running:

1. Right-click My Computer and choose Manage. The My Computer icon is probably on the desktop and/or the Start menu.

2. Under Computer Management (Local), expand Services And Applications.

3. Click Indexing Service. The results are shown in Figure 2-10. (Notice that the items under the Indexing Service are also expanded in this screen shot. This is simply for reference later.)

If you don't see anything in the Size column (on the title bar in the right pane) or any of the other columns to the right of it, the service is not running.

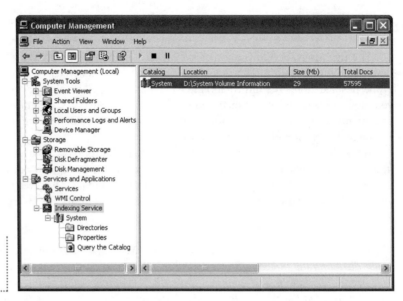

FIGURE 2-10 The
Computer Management
console and the
Indexing Service

To start the service, click Action | Start. (You can also use the DVD-type icons on the menu bar.) To stop the service, right-click Indexing Service and click Stop.

As shown in Figure 2-10, the items directly under the Indexing Service are the catalogs. Catalogs hold the indexed information. By default, there is one, System, as shown in Figure 2-10. You can add additional catalogs from the Action menu. The System catalog has two subfolders, Directories and Properties, and an option to query the catalog. Directories are created when the indexing is done, and can include folders for Documents and Settings and for entire drives. You can create new directories from the Action menu. including information such as the date the document was created, the author name, the document's size, and more. If you decide that you can use and benefit from the Indexing Service, you'll want to learn quite a bit more about it. To do so, in the Computer Management console, select Indexing Service and click Help | Help Topics.

Query the Catalog

If you decide to use the Indexing Service, you'll want to learn the ways to query it.

To locate a specific document on your hard drive, you use the Indexing Service's query language. Using this language, you can search for documents based on specific words in the document, or even phrases. You can search by author name, document size, or even the document's ActiveX properties, such as its summary. There are five types of queries:

- **Free-text** You input single words or a group of words, such as a sentence. The Indexing Service finds documents with the same meaning, and not necessarily the exact sentence. Think of it as searching using a web engine, without using quotation marks around your search words.

- **Phrase** You input a phrase you believe to be in a document. Putting quotes around this tells the service to locate the exact phrase.

- **Pattern-matching** You input wildcards, denoted by asterisks, to tell the service you want to search for files that contain patterns. For instance, you can search for *.xls to locate all of the Microsoft Excel spreadsheet files on the computer.

- **Relational** You input the words you want to search for, and then add Boolean operators such as And, Or, Not, Near, and =. The results are sorted in relation to how you input the operators.

- **Vector space** You input specific words or phrases you want to find in a document, and then decide how much "weight" you want each of the words or phrases to be assigned. There is no easy way to input this information, and queries look something like this:

  book, {weight value=.3} cover, {weight value=.3} Hard Core, {weight value=.4}

Once you've decided on what type of query you want, you need to input it. You can search using the query language from the Search option or from inside the Computer Management console. Since you're likely already in the console, you can practice from there. You need to know some rules before you get started, many of which are also applied when searching with a web browser and looking for something on the Internet:

- The search data you input is not case sensitive.

- Some words are automatically omitted from searches, and they are all common words: all, as, be, but, did, he, them, to, too, very, and your.

- If you must use a character in a query, such as &, #, or @ (and there are others), enclose those in parentheses so the service does not think they are operators or wildcards.

- The best form in which to input dates and times is yyyy/mm/dd and hh:mm:ss.

■ You can use tags to construct queries, which are indicated by braces, { }. Tags are used in long form queries; when tags are not used, it is referred to as the short form.

■ The @ sign is used to introduce a phrase query. Examples are @filename=*.xls (all file names created with Microsoft Excel or with that file extension), @DocTitle"Hard Core XP" (any file with the title Hard Core XP).

■ & means *and*, | means *or*, and ! means *not*. These symbols are used in Boolean queries such as hard & core (contains both words), book | cover (contains either word), and book ! picture (contains book but not picture).

The Indexing Service Query Language is quite complex, and what I've introduced here is only the beginning. To see more details regarding this language, consult the Windows XP Help and Support pages. Figure 2-11 shows a sample query and the one of nine results this query supplies.

FIGURE 2-11 Query results

APPLYING NTFS COMPRESSION AND ENCRYPTION

Hopefully, your computer is now running faster and more efficiently. Now it's time to make it a little more secure. Although NTFS compression and encryption can't be found in the Services console, and you can't open them from the All Programs or Accessories menus, I still consider them to be a type of service and have thus made the decision to include them in this chapter. Both compression and encryption are a convenience to users, the former for allowing the user to condense a file or folder to save disk space or to archive old data, and the latter for securing the data stored on the computer.

 Encryption, as is also true for Remote Desktop, Offline Files and Folders, Multiprocessor Support, Group Policy, Remote Installation Services, and Roaming User Profiles, isn't available in Windows XP Home Edition.

NTFS compression and encryption are usually discussed together, as they are here. There are a few reasons for this, namely that both require you to have an NTFS-formatted hard drive, and both can be denoted with color in Windows Explorer (as described at the end of this chapter). Both are also applied using a file's or folder's advanced properties. Each does completely different things, though, and each has its own built-in limitations.

↘ Increase Disk Space with NTFS Compression

NTFS compression decreases file and folder size, and reduces the amount of space required on your hard drive for storing data.

Compression can be used for single files or folders, or for an entire drive. Although compression can save on the amount of disk space required to store data, compressing files may cause the computer to slow down while it compresses and decompresses the data. Windows XP's compression utility is one that works all the time, in the background, compressing and decompressing the folder or file automatically each time you open, use, and close it. (You don't have to "agree" to anything beforehand, or work through any wizard.)

To use XP's built-in compression, do the following:

1. Open My Computer, select a drive that contains data you rarely use, and locate the folder or drive to compress. From any drive, you could consider compressing a folder that contains old files, such as a subfolder of My Documents or My Pictures, or a folder that you created that contains a backup of archived data.

2. Right-click the file, folder, or drive, and click Properties.

3. On the General tab, click Advanced.

4. From the Advanced Attributes dialog box, check Compress Contents To Save Disk Space, as shown in Figure 2-12, and click OK. Click OK twice more to verify the command. Note that you can apply the changes to the folder and all subfolders during the verification.

FIGURE 2-12 Compress folders or drives

If you can't compress the drive or data, you might not have an NTFS-formatted hard drive. To find out, and to convert the drive:

1. Right-click My Computer and choose Manage.

2. In the Computer Management console, expand Storage, and select Disk Management.

3. View each of the disks on your system. Figure 2-13 shows two disks, both formatted as NTFS.

4. If the disk is not formatted as NTFS, but is instead FAT or FAT 32, open a command prompt from Start | All Programs | Accessories, and type **convert** *c***: /fs:ntfs**, where *c* is the letter of the drive to convert.

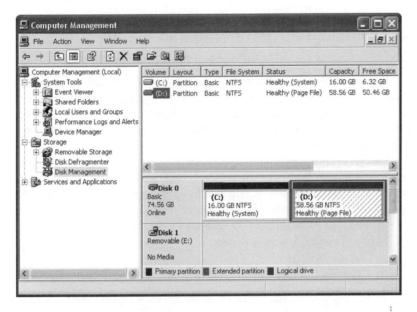

FIGURE 2-13 NTFS drives

Don't Confuse NTFS Compression with Compressed Folders

NTFS compression is often confused with Compressed (Zipped) Folders. They are not the same. Compressed (Zipped) Folders is an option available by right-clicking a file or folder and is included in the Send To menu. This utility also compresses data, but works more like WinZip or Stuff It. It creates a new, zipped file that you can move data in and out of as desired. If you've already downloaded and installed a third-party compression utility, you'll be prompted to designate Compressed (Zipped) Folders as the application for handling the compressed files each time you use it.

Compressed (Zipped) folders take up less space than uncompressed folders, and can be used on drives formatted with FAT as well as NTFS. You can also assign passwords to these zipped files, and unzip them with third-party programs. Compressed (Zipped) Folders is a good option when e-mailing or archiving small amounts of data. These types of compressed folders have no effect on hard drive performance.

Protect Your Data with Encryption

Encryption can be used to further secure data on the computer.

Encryption, another option available in a file, folder, or drive's Advanced Attributes dialog box, allows you to encode the contents of the designated item. Only the user who encrypts the file can decrypt it, and encryption can be performed only on NTFS volumes. Encrypting a compressed folder causes it to lose its compression.

Encryption is a good option for those who share a computer with others, or for people who carry a laptop regularly and thus are at a greater risk of having it stolen. Encryption is achieved by applying an algorithm, and only the person with the correct "key" can unlock the code. This is all done in the background, and has no effect on a computer's performance.

To encrypt a file, folder, or drive:

1. Open My Computer and locate the folder or drive to encrypt.

2. Right-click the file, folder, or drive, and click Properties.

3. On the General tab, click Advanced.

4. In the Advanced Attributes dialog box, check Encrypt Contents To Secure Data and click OK. Click OK twice more to close the dialog boxes.

You can copy and move encrypted files just as you would any other files. The only problem you'll encounter is if you copy or move an encrypted file or folder to a non-NTFS volume. If this happens, encryption will be lost.

Finally, encrypting a file doesn't make it bullet-proof. The file can still be deleted, and the data lost. It's important to protect important data using a number of security features, and not rely solely on encryption. As an example, applying NTFS permissions, using password protection, configuring password requirements and password lockout periods, and using a firewall and antivirus software will all help protect valuable data.

Change the Color of Compressed, Encrypted Folders

After compressed and encrypted files, folders, and drives have been created, you can denote those in Windows Explorer with color.

Changing the color of compressed or encrypted files allows you to find them faster and keep data more organized. To do this:

1. Right-click Start and click Explore All Users.

2. Click Tools | Folder Options.

3. On the View tab, scroll down to the bottom of the Advanced Settings and check Show Encrypted Or Compressed NTFS Files In Color, as shown in Figure 2-14.

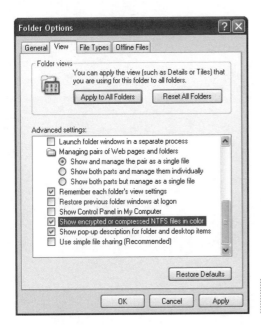

FIGURE 2-14 Mark encrypted and compressed files in color

4. Click OK.

Now that you've discovered how to enhance your computer by using the Program Compatibility Wizard and disabling services you don't need, you are ready to move forward and learn how to enhance and increase performance of your e-mail and Internet activities. In the next chapter, you'll learn how to use Outlook Express to back up and restore data, how to control spam, and how to get more out of your overall Internet experience.

CHAPTER 3
E-MAIL AND THE WEB

You can increase performance and get more out of e-mailing and the Internet if you know a few tips and tricks. One of the tips in this chapter involves backing up and restoring data, including archiving e-mail messages, in Outlook Express. For some reason, Microsoft has made this seemingly simple task a difficult one. There are other ways to increase your Outlook Express experience as well, including creating identities for everyone who uses the program, learning tricks for controlling spam, and knowing how to organize the data you want to keep.

There are ways to enhance your Internet Explorer web browser too. For instance, you can enable Content Advisor to protect your children from harmful content while they are surfing the Web, use group policies to control how Internet Explorer works for all users, and use options in Internet Explorer to erase information about the sites you've visited. You can even tell Internet Explorer not to save your passwords. All of these things will enhance your Internet experience, by keeping it safe and personalizing it to suit your needs.

But What If I Use Outlook?

You may also use Outlook, the full version of Outlook Express, either at work or at home. Outlook is part of the Microsoft Office 2003 suite of applications, available for purchase at your local computer store. Since Outlook does not come with Windows XP by default, I won't discuss it here. However, if you aren't getting what you need from Outlook Express, you should consider it.

Microsoft Outlook offers many additional features, including the following:

- Junk e-mail filtering

- Desktop alerts for appointments

- Calendar

- Grammar-checking tools

- Collaboration tools

- Hundreds of organizational options for incoming and saved e-mail

Additionally, you can go to Microsoft's web site, search for Outlook Downloads, and obtain a myriad of free stuff, including service packs, personal folders backup software, stationary, and more.

OUTLOOK EXPRESS

Outlook Express is a program that ships with Windows XP for sending and receiving e-mail. Unbeknownst to many, though, its capabilities go much deeper than that. You can organize data that you keep, and you can have messages sent to specific folders as they arrive in your Inbox. Let's start with organizing then, and creating folders for archiving messages you want to keep.

⇘ Super-Charge Outlook Express by Organizing Your Data

Creating folders and moving data into them is the easiest way to clean up your Inbox.

If you've ever had more than 50 e-mail messages in your Inbox, you need to do some serious organizing. Those 50 e-mails not only clutter up your Inbox, but can cause you to feel overwhelmed and make it difficult to focus on what you actually need to do. All those e-mails make opening Outlook Express take longer too, and may even cause it to become overtaxed and close unexpectedly. By creating folders, you can move those messages out of your Inbox to a more manageable and suitable area. Figure 3-1 shows a typical Outlook Express setup, with lots of folders created to manage messages.

The Inbox shown in Figure 3-1 has, among others, two folders for clients (Clients 2003-2004, Clients 2004-2005), a folder for this book (Hard Core Windows XP), and another named Ongoing, which contains several subfolders that hold e-mail that needs to be kept for future reference, and e-mail for ongoing projects. You can supercharge your own Outlook Express by creating some hierarchy that's similar.

Once you decide what folders you need and what type of folder hierarchy to use, you can create folders quite easily:

1. Open Outlook Express and access your Inbox. You can locate Outlook Express in the All Programs menu. (If you use the Welcome screen, click Inbox.)

2. If necessary, expand Local Folders.

3. Right-click Local Folders and select New Folder.

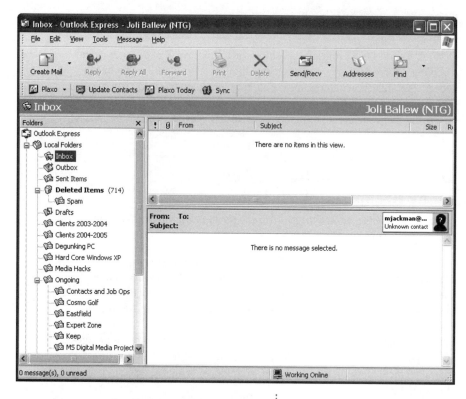

FIGURE 3-1 A typical Outlook Express folder management layout

4. In the Create Folder dialog box, type a name for the folder. An example is shown in Figure 3-2.

5. To create the new folder under the Local Folders tree, click OK. To create the folder in another folder (as a subfolder), select that folder before selecting OK.

With folders created, you can now drag and drop any message from any folder to the newly created ones. Simply select the e-mail to move, and drag and drop it into the desired folder for storage. Once you have created folders and moved e-mails into them, you can select View | Layout to hide those folders from view if you don't need to view them all the time.

You can select multiple, consecutive messages by holding down the SHIFT key and selecting the first and last messages to move in a list, or you can select nonconsecutive messages by holding down the CTRL key while selecting.

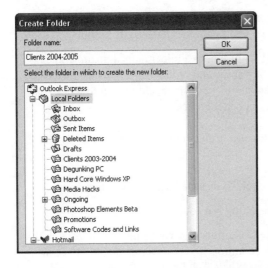

FIGURE 3-2 Create folders to manage data

↘ You Rule the Roost: Assigning Rules to Your E-Mails

Message rules tell Outlook Express what to do with incoming e-mail, and can help you organize your Inbox.

After creating folders, you can create message rules so that e-mail that meets specific criteria goes to a folder automatically, relieving you from having to move it manually. Having e-mail skip the Inbox and go directly to a specific folder can be beneficial in a number of ways. It keeps your Inbox free of clutter, and it helps you automatically organize the mail you get. If you're looking for ideas for folder creation, try these on for size:

- ■ Route e-mail from e-mail communities directly to a specific folder named after the community. You can read it at your leisure, and your Inbox stays uncluttered.

- ■ Route e-mail from your spouse directly to a folder named Spouse. You'll see that there's unread e-mail in the folder because it is denoted by a number next to the folder (and you can get to it when the boss isn't looking).

- ■ Have e-mail with FW in the Subject line go directly to a folder named FW. (Most FWs are jokes, updates, and nonemergency e-mails. Just don't forget to check it once a day.)

■ CC yourself on important e-mails to bosses or coworkers, and have the e-mail you receive sent to a folder named CC to Me.

■ Have e-mail deemed spam sent to a folder named Spam. You can always check the folder at the end of the day, and locate misplaced messages. You can create rules for spam, although a separate spam-filtering application is a better choice.

Once you know what rules you want to create, it's fairly easy to create them:

1. In Outlook Express, click Tools | Message Rules | Mail.

2. In the Message Rules dialog box, click New.

3. In the area Select The Conditions For Your Rule, scroll through the choices and choose a condition. To create a rule that has to do with a specific person, select Where The From Line Contains People. To create a rule that has to do with specific words in the message of an e-mail (such as common words in spam you receive), select Where The Message Body Contains Specific Words. If you're unsure of what any choice means, click the question mark in the top-right corner and click again on the item for which you need help.

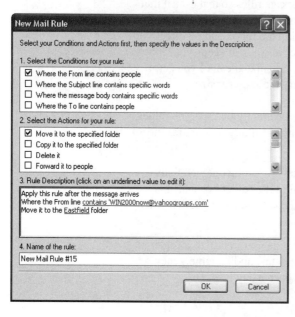

FIGURE 3-3   Create a message rule

4. In the Select The Actions For Your Rule area, choose an action to perform. To move the e-mail to a specific folder, check Move It To The Specified Folder. To delete it, check Delete It. Scroll through the choices to see others.

5. In the third section, Rule Description, click on each area in blue to configure the settings. These options will change depending on what you've chosen in Steps 3 and 4, but for the most part, you'll be required to make other selections from other dialog boxes. Figure 3-3 shows a completed message rule.

6. In the fourth section, Name Of The Rule, type a descriptive name for the rule and click OK to apply it.

◥ Keep Your Own Identity

If someone shares your Address Book and Outlook Express, create a separate identity for them.

Your Outlook Express identity is what defines how you work with Outlook Express, from how your folders are organized to how your message rules are configured. Having separate identities for those who share Outlook Express (such as other family members) allows each person to see their own mail and contacts, create their own folder hierarchy, have their own e-mail address, and more.

You might even want to create multiple identities for yourself, especially if you use the same computer for work and play. You could configure one identity you use from nine to five, and another identity you use once your work is complete. With a separate identity, you can also keep separate your work and play e-mail addresses.

To create a new identity and configure it for yourself, another family member, or coworker:

1. From inside Outlook Express, click File | Identities | Add New Identity.

2. In the New Identity dialog box, shown in Figure 3-4, type a name for the new identity and, if desired, check Require A Password.

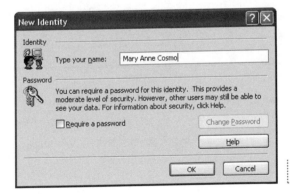

FIGURE 3-4 Create a new identity

3. Click OK.

4. When prompted to switch to the new identity, click OK. If prompted to keep the active connection to the Internet, click Yes.

5. When prompted to set up a new mail account, choose either Create A New Internet Mail Account or Use An Existing Internet Mail Account. Your choice will determine how the procedure continues. If you choose to create a new Internet mail account, you are prompted to input all relevant information from your Internet service provider (ISP). If you choose to use an existing account, you have the option of verifying the information as it is already input.

6. When prompted to import messages and an Address Book, decide whether or not you want to import. If you choose to import, you'll be given the choice to import both messages and the Address Book, messages only, or the Address Book only, as shown in Figure 3-5.

FIGURE 3-5 Choose what to import

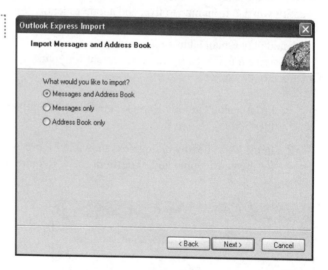

7. Click Next to continue through the wizard to complete the import process.

8. To switch back to the original identity, click File | Switch Identities.

◥ Back Up and Restore E-Mail

Outlook Express doesn't come with a way to automatically back up messages, folders, and the Address Book on a schedule, so you have to do those tasks manually.

Most people think about backing up their documents, pictures, music, and video on occasion but they never even consider backing up their e-mail messages and Address Book. Perhaps that's because there's no easy way to back up these items on a regular basis. There's no easy way to drag and drop e-mail data to a backup drive, as you can do with data stored in default folders. Backing up e-mail messages may be just as important as backing up other data, though, especially if you depend on your e-mail for your livelihood. You never know when you may have to go back and retrieve a long-ago sent e-mail or locate a software registration code. In addition, if you have a complete meltdown with no record of your address book, you're going to have a hard time letting your contacts know about it!

 If more than one identity exists in Outlook Express, these procedures must be performed for each of them.

To copy e-mail messages to a backup folder:

1. Open Outlook Express and click Tools | Options.

2. On the Maintenance tab, click Store Folder.

3. Use the mouse to select the Store Location.

4. Right-click the location, as shown in Figure 3-6, and select Copy.

FIGURE 3-6 Copy the store location

5. Click Cancel, and click Cancel again to close the Options dialog box.

6. Click Start | Run, right-click inside the Open text box, and select Paste. Click OK.

7. In the window that opens, click Edit | Select All.

8. With the folders selected, Click Edit | Copy. Close this window.

9. Open Windows Explorer and browse to the area where you want to create the backup. This may be a backup drive, a networked computer, or writeable media.

10. Right-click an empty area in the backup area window and click New | Folder. Name the folder **Mail Backup**, followed by the date.

11. Open the new folder, and click Edit | Paste.

12. Once the copy is complete, the backup is done.

To export the Address Book to a file:

1. Open Outlook Express and click File | Export | Address Book.

2. Select Text File (Comma Separated Values), and click Export.

3. Click Browse, and navigate in the CSV Export dialog box to the backup folder you created earlier, when creating a folder for messages.

4. In the File Name drop-down box, type **Address Book** followed by the date, and click Save.

5. Click Next in the CSV Export dialog box.

6. Select the items to back up, as shown in Figure 3-7.

FIGURE 3-7 Select items to back up

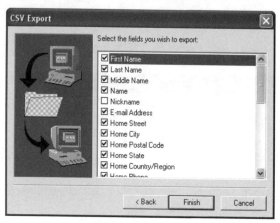

7. Click Finish, click OK, and then click Close.

To import messages from the backup folder:

1. In Outlook Express, click File | Import | Messages.

2. In the Outlook Express Import dialog box, select Microsoft Outlook Express 6, and click Next.

3. Select Import Mail From An OE6 Store Directory and click OK.

4. Click Browse, and locate the folder that contains the mail backup.

5. Click OK, and then click Next.

6. Click All Folders, click Next, and then click Finish.

To import the Address Book file:

1. In Outlook Express, click File | Import | Other Address Book.

2. Click Text File (Comma Separated Values), and click Import.

3. Click Browse, and locate the backup of the Address Book created earlier. Select it and click Open.

4. Click Next, click Finish, click OK, and then click Close.

➥ Even Your Account Settings Need Attention

Outlook Express doesn't come with a way to automatically back up mail account settings, so you have to do it manually.

Now that you've backed up your e-mail messages and Address Book, you should take one more step and back up your e-mail account information. If your computer crashes and you have to restore that data, it will be available. There's nothing worse than trying to remember the information for your e-mail servers (are they POP3 or HTTP?) or waiting on hold with your ISP for hours just to reconfigure your e-mail address and account information.

 If more than one identity exists in Outlook Express, these procedures must be performed for each of them.

To make a backup of your Outlook Express mail account settings and export the mail account information to a file:

1. In Outlook Express, click Tools | Accounts.

2. In the Internet Accounts dialog box, shown in Figure 3-8, click the Mail tab, select the account you want to back up the settings for, and click Export.

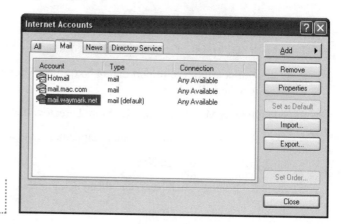

FIGURE 3-8   Select the account to export

3. Browse to the location of the previously created backup folder, accept the default name for the file, and click Save.

4. Repeat for any other accounts. Click Close when finished.

 As always, repeat these steps for multiple identities.

To import the mail account file:

1. In Outlook Express, click Tools | Accounts.

2. On the Mail tab, click Import.

3. In the Look In box, browse to the location of the backup folder created earlier.

4. Select the account to import, and click Open.

5. Click Close.

↘ Slam Spam

Spam is unwanted e-mail; learn how to avoid it and what to do when it takes hold.

Spam, as you are probably all too aware, is e-mail sent by a solicitor to try to entice you to buy something from their company. Most spam involves items you don't want, like enhancement or performance drugs, prescription drugs, mortgage offers, pornography, and travel offers. Although some spam comes from companies you trust, the vast majority does not. You might get unwanted e-mail from companies you've registered with, such as after purchasing a new refrigerator or computer, or accepting a credit card offer through the mail. Almost always, spam is a menace, and is not desired by its recipient.

Once spammers get a hold of your e-mail address, they'll never let go. They'll continue to send spam from all over the world, and circulate your address to other spammers for a small fee. The best way to deal with spam, then, is to avoid it in the first place. Here are some suggestions:

- Get a Hotmail account from **http://www.hotmail.com** and use it whenever you need to register to access a web site, purchase items online, or register with a company for warranty services. This address can be deleted and a new one created if the spammers take it over. Hotmail also does a great job of filtering spam, which is another reason it is an excellent choice.

- Tell friends and family not to add you to their "forwarding jokes" list, and not to share your address with anyone else.

- If you join a newsgroup, use your Hotmail address, or use your real one and include words such as REMOVETHIS, NOSPAM, or something similar in the message that you send to join the newsgroup.

- Don't unsubscribe from spam messages—by doing so, you just let the spammers know your address is a working one.

If you find yourself buried in spam, meaning you're getting 25+ spam messages a day, you need to take further action. There are several spam filtering utilities available on the Internet, and your ISP may offer options for controlling spam as well. Yahoo! lets you denote messages as spam, and then Yahoo! uses the information from clients to perfect its filters. Other companies have similar options. To find spam filtering programs, either visit your local computer store or search on **http://www.google.com** for Spam Filter. There are several free options.

You can also create a folder specifically for spam, create message rules, and send messages that meet specific criteria to those folders (refer to "You Rule the Roost: Assigning Rules to Your E-Mails," earlier in the chapter). You may, for instance, create a message rule that lists words found in spam messages, like Viagra, Via|gra, Vi|agra, etc., and have e-mail that contains these words directed automatically to the Spam folder. This strategy is difficult to keep up with, though, because spammers figure out right away ways to get around these rules.

You can also use the Block Sender command. This also is not as desirable as a third-party spam filtering utility, but it can help some. When spam comes in, add the spammer to the Blocked Senders List, and if any more e-mail comes from that particular e-mail address, you won't receive it in your Inbox. To add a sender to the Blocked Senders List:

1. Open Outlook Express and select the message deemed spam.

2. Click Message | Block Sender.

3. Click Yes to verify and to remove all messages from the sender.

 You can also click Message | Create Rule From Message to create a specific rule for that sender.

If you accidentally block a sender or no longer want to block someone on the list, here's how to remove them from your blocked list:

1. Open Outlook Express.

2. Click Tools | Message Rules | Blocked Senders List.

3. Choose the Blocked Senders tab, and uncheck any sender you no longer wish to block. Click OK.

EXPLORING INTERNET EXPLORER

Internet Explorer is the web browser that ships with Windows XP and is the web browser most XP users prefer and use. Internet Explorer allows you to visit any web page on the Internet; download applications, music, photos, and video; purchase merchandise online; and access newsgroups and web communities. As with any software, though, there are tweaks you can perform to personalize it and make it safer to use, for you, your company, and your children.

⬆ Use Content Advisor to Advise You About Content

Content Advisor lets you set rating levels for language, nudity, sex, and/or violence, and will then deny access to web content that contains content that you deem objectionable.

If I had to guess, I'd say one of the least used options in Internet Explorer is Content Advisor. Content Advisor enables you to control what kinds of material can be viewed, based on ratings you define. These settings can help you protect both yourself and your family from questionable and objectionable material.

To access and enable Content Advisor:

1. Open Internet Explorer and click Tools | Internet Options.

2. Click the Content tab to view the Content Advisor choices, as shown in Figure 3-9.

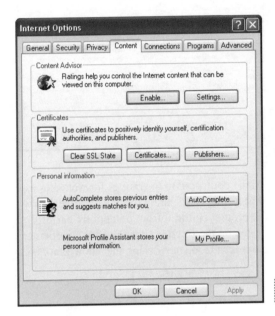

FIGURE 3-9 Locate Content Advisor

3. Click Enable, and click OK in the Content Advisor dialog box that appears.

4. When prompted, create a password and password hint and click OK.

5. Click OK again to verify you are enabling Content Advisor.

6. To configure Content Advisor, click Settings, input your password, and click OK.

7. The Ratings tab, shown in Figure 3-10, is where you configure the options for language, nudity, sex, and violence. Highlight each and move the slider appropriately.

8. Click OK when finished.

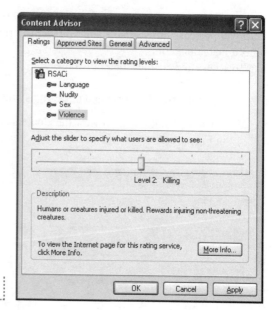

FIGURE 3-10 Configure Content Advisor

The ratings you choose will be compared to the ratings for web sites as assigned by the Internet Content Rating Association, or ICRA (**http://www .icra.org/about/**). Its aim is to protect children from potentially harmful material and to protect free speech on the Internet. If ratings for a particular site are not up to your set standards in Content Advisor, the site will not be viewable.

⬊ Erase History

Internet Explorer's History option keeps a list of recently viewed web sites.

If you're not sure if you need to configure Internet Explorer to prevent access to objectionable web content using Content Advisor, take a quick peek at what's been recently viewed on your computer. Using Internet Explorer's History option, you can see data that details what sites users who access your computer (think kids, coworkers, or spouses) have visited. You may decide to use Content Advisor after all, or even purchase a third-party content-filtering utility like NetNanny.

If at some point your users get a clue that you're looking at the History list, and start clearing it when they exit the program, you can use a Group Policy tweak to prevent them from doing that. You can also protect *yourself* by deleting the History log as *you* exit, or prevent the History from being created at all.

Let's see what's in the History list first. To see the last three weeks' worth of web sites that have been visited using your computer and Internet Explorer:

1. Open Internet Explorer.

2. Click View | Explorer Bar | History.

3. As shown in Figure 3-11, you can expand any day and any web site to see what sites and pages were viewed and when. If you didn't view the page, it means someone else did.

To clear the History list on exit and/or to prevent History from being created:

1. Open Internet Explorer.

2. Click Tools | Internet Options.

3. On the General tab, click Clear History, and then click Yes to verify you want to clear the History list.

4. To prevent the History from being created at all, change Days To Keep Pages In History to 0.

FIGURE 3-11 The History list shows recent activity.

 You can also change the default number of days (21) to keep pages in History, and configure it for up to 99 days.

If you have Windows XP Professional (and I've been assuming you do while writing this book), you can prevent users from changing the History settings in Internet Explorer by using Group Policy. If you have XP Home Edition, you'll have to purchase a third-party tool to do this. To prevent all users from tampering with History settings and thus deleting their History on exit in Windows XP Professional:

1. Click Start | Run.

2. In the Open list box, type **gpedit.msc**.

3. Expand User Configuration | Administrative Templates | Windows Components | Internet Explorer, and locate Disable Changing History Settings.

4. Double-click that option and select Enabled.

The settings in the History area on the General tab in the Internet Options dialog box will not be available, and will be grayed out, as shown in Figure 3-12.

FIGURE 3-12 Disable access to History settings

 Web activity can also be traced by looking at the items in the Temporary Files Folder. I'll talk about that later in this chapter.

↘ Get Rid of (and Avoid) Spyware and Adware

You might not know it, but your computer may be infected with spyware or adware.

Spyware is a term that is often used interchangeably with advertising supported software, or adware, but they are not the same. Spyware is a technology that allows people or organizations to acquire information about a person without their knowledge. This information, which generally contains data about the person's buying habits, when and what sites they visit, and, occasionally, personal information, can also take the form of a virus and is often spread through downloads like the free version of KaZaa. Adware is also a software application, but it is less destructive. Adware applications generally install reminder notifications or target specific ads at you when you surf the Internet. Adware tailors pop-ups to your buying habits, based on what the adware has learned about you while you've been surfing.

If you have downloaded suspicious material, visited not-so-reputable web sites, clicked banner ads, or used file-sharing web sites illegally, you may have spyware, adware, or both on your computer. Even if you haven't done any of these activities, you should check your computer for the software anyway. There are several free programs, but Ad-Aware and OptOut are my two favorites. Both are freeware and check your computer for suspected spyware programs.

To obtain and use Ad-Aware to check for suspicious programs on your computer:

1. Visit **http://www.lavasoft.nu/** and, on the left side of the page, click Ad-Aware Personal. This version is free for noncommercial use.

2. Click the Download button and choose a download site from which to download the software.

3. When prompted, click Save, and save the download to your hard drive. Verify that Close This Dialog Box When Download Completes is not checked.

4. When the download completes, as shown in Figure 3-13, click Open, and follow the instructions to install the program.

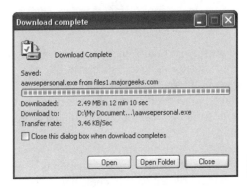

FIGURE 3-13 Click Open to install

5. Once the program is installed, verify that Perform A Full System Scan Now and Update Definition File Now are selected and click Finish.

6. Wait while the scan is performed. Sample results are shown in Figure 3-14.

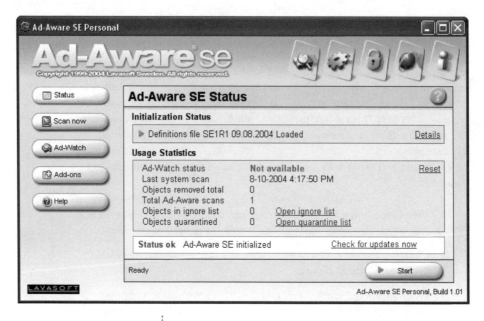

FIGURE 3-14 Sample Ad-Aware results

⬊ Surf in Secret

There are lots of ways to cover your tracks while surfing the Web.

If you're into your privacy and want to surf the Web without leaving any tracks, you'll likely need third-party tools to do that successfully. There are a few things you can tweak in Internet Explorer, though, such as deleting the History on exit, as detailed in an earlier tip. The other tweaks all are accessible in Internet Explorer from the Internet Options dialog box (available from the Tools menu):

■ From the General tab, you can delete cookies and/or temporary Internet files. Cookies are text files placed on your computer by the web sites you visit, and they store information about your preferences when you visit. Temporary Internet files store graphics and web pages as you view them, so the next time you visit the site, the information will be cached and load faster. Both can give information about your surfing habits to those who also have access to your computer and know where and how to look for private information.

■ From the Content tab, you can disable AutoComplete. AutoComplete lists possible matches for your partially typed web addresses, forms, usernames, and passwords. Disabling this will help maintain your privacy when others are accessing your computer. If you have AutoComplete on, any user can simply type in a couple of letters of your user name, if they can guess it, and a password will often appear automatically.

■ From the Security tab, you can create custom levels of security using the Custom Level button and configuring options in the resulting Security Settings dialog box. Here, you can disable, enable, or be prompted when ActiveX controls and plug-ins are run; enable, disable, or prompt for downloads; and require user authentication just to name a few of the many options.

■ From the Privacy tab, you can override automatic cookie handling, by choosing to accept, block, or prompt first- and third-party cookies.

Let's take a look at those options and tabs:

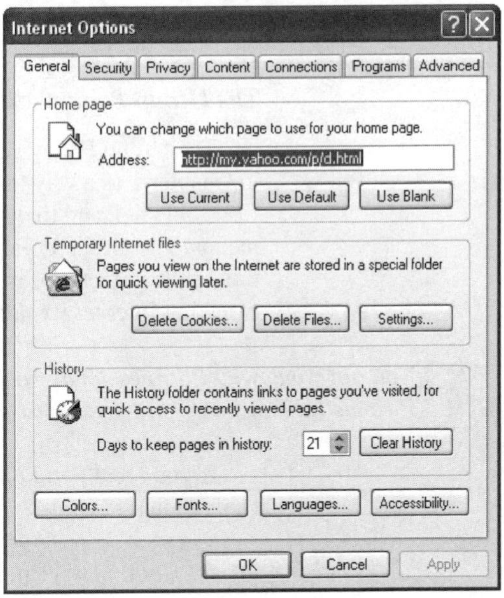

1. Open Internet Explorer and click Tools | Internet Options. The General tab of the Internet Options dialog box is shown in Figure 3-15.

2. Click Delete Cookies and then click Yes to verify that you want to delete the cookies from your machine. Keep in mind that if you do this, you won't be recognized by the web sites you frequent, and you'll have to set preferences again if desired.

3. Click Delete Files to delete temporary Internet files. These files can take up quite a bit of space on your hard drive, and should be deleted every couple of months, just to "clean house."

FIGURE 3-15 The General tab of Internet Options

FIGURE 3-16 Disable AutoComplete for privacy and security

4. Click the Content tab, click AutoComplete, and uncheck any items you don't want automatically completed while you're surfing the Web. Notice that you can also clear forms and passwords from the cache. Figure 3-16 shows an example.

5. Click OK to exit out of the dialog boxes.

The Security and Privacy tabs are a little more complex, and since security will be covered in Chapter 5, refer to that chapter for a complete rundown.

If you find that you need more security than this, and really want to remain anonymous on the Web, consider third-party applications. My favorites include SurfSecret Privacy Protector, available at **http://www.surfsecret.com/**, Top Secret Crypto Gold, available at **http://www.topsecretcrypto.com/**, and Internet Eraser Pro, available at **http://www.interneteraser.com/detail.html**.

⬃ Tweak IE Even More with the Group Policy Editor

The Group Policy Editor offers additional Internet Explorer tweaks.

The Group Policy Editor in Windows XP Professional was introduced in Chapter 1 as a way to personalize the Desktop, the Start menu, and the Control Panel, and to disable items such as balloon tips or personalized menus. The Group Policy Editor offers many more options, though, thousands in fact, and in this section, you learn about the options for tweaking Internet Explorer.

 If you run Windows XP Professional, you have the Group Policy Editor. If you have Windows XP Home Edition, you won't be able to use this tip.

If you recall, you open the Group Policy Editor in Windows XP Professional like this:

1. Click Start | Run.

2. Type **gpedit.msc** in the Open window, and click OK.

3. To access the Internet Explorer settings, expand User Configuration | Administrative Templates | Windows Components, and then select Internet Explorer, as shown in Figure 3-17.

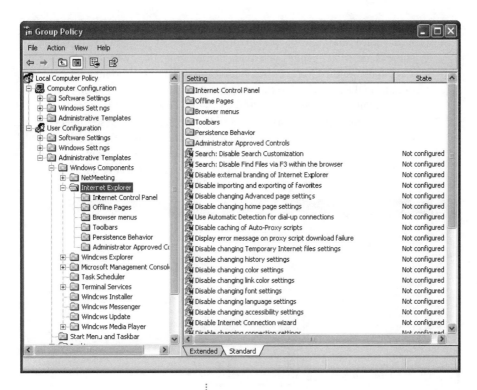

FIGURE 3-17 Internet Explorer options in the Group Policy Editor

Earlier you learned how to prevent users from changing the History settings in Internet Explorer. As you can see in Figure 3-17, there are several other options too (all located in the same pane):

- Disable importing and exporting of Favorites

- Disable changing home page settings

- Disable changing accessibility settings

- Disable changing connection settings

- Disable changing ratings settings

- Do not allow AutoComplete to save passwords

There are more settings, and you can browse those at your leisure. Each setting has an explanation of what happens if you enable or disable it, too, making it almost foolproof. The only thing to watch out for is that you must remember what you've changed. For example, two years from now you may need to use AutoComplete for forms. If you have disabled it, you might have a hard time figuring out why it won't work if you don't write down somewhere what changes you made in the Group Policy Editor.

Finally, in the Group Policy Editor, browse through the Internet Explorer options in the six available folders (also shown in Figure 3-17): Internet Control Panel, Offline Pages, Browser Menus, Toolbars, Persistence Behavior, and Administrator Approved Controls. Each of these folders offers even more tweaks, as shown in Figure 3-18, which shows the options for Browser Menus; notice the option selected, Hide Favorites Menu. Tweak to your heart's content. When you're finished, close the Group Policy Editor.

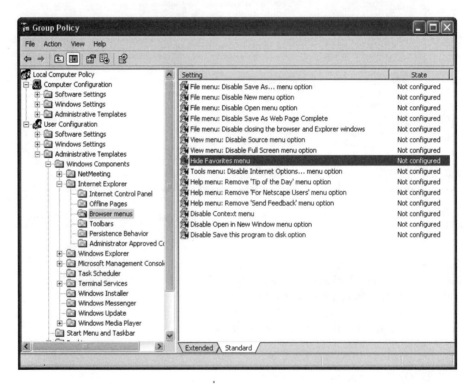

FIGURE 3-18 More tweaks with Group Policy Editor

In this chapter, you learned some tricks for personalizing Outlook Express and Internet Explorer and getting them to work to your advantage. That's a good start, but in the next chapter, you'll learn even more about what can be done over the Internet. For one, you'll learn how you can use Windows XP to work from home, and how to give and get remote assistance over the Internet without ever leaving your office. If you have a laptop and an office computer, you can work from almost anywhere in the world!

CHAPTER 4
WORKING REMOTELY

Working remotely means being able to access your desktop computer from anywhere, whether you are accessing your work computer from your desktop computer at home, accessing the company servers by using your laptop from a motel room, or accessing a remote computer in some other scenario. When working remotely, you are connected to the remote computer and can access its icons, shortcuts, files, folders, and programs, just as if you were sitting in front of it. Distance doesn't matter.

There are lots of ways to work remotely with Windows XP. You can give and get remote assistance, connect remotely to your own computer or someone else's using Remote Desktop, and interact with people across the world or across the office using NetMeeting. These three technologies are introduced in this chapter, along with tips for getting the most out of them, and for securing the computer while doing so.

REMOTE ASSISTANCE: TAPPING INTO YOUR FRIENDS FOR HELP

Remote Assistance is a technology that allows users to ask for and receive computer help from friends and family, coworkers, network administrators, and IT departments, without having to have someone physically visit them at their machine. Remote Assistance lets you invite someone you trust to help you troubleshoot your computer or learn a new skill. The person you choose will be able to view your screen from their monitor, chat with you, and, if you give them permission, even take control of your computer using their own mouse and keyboard. And it doesn't matter how far away they are!

There are a few prerequisites for choosing a helper, though, and all of the following terms must be met:

- Both parties must be using Windows XP.

- Both parties must have Outlook Express, Microsoft Outlook, or Windows Messenger.

- Both parties must be connected to the Internet.

- Both parties, if also a part of a local area network (LAN), must have permission to use Remote Assistance from their network administrators.

- Both parties must be willing to participate in the Remote Assistance session.

 Never agree to a Remote Assistance session from someone you don't know. They could infect your computer with a virus or obtain personal information.

Ask and You Shall Receive: Getting Remote Assistance

If you need assistance, you can ask for it using the Remote Assistance option in Help and Support.

It's easy to get free computer assistance from colleagues or friends; simply click Invite Someone To Help You, choose a Windows Messenger buddy or an e-mail contact, and wait for them to respond. Once they respond, you'll use the Remote Assistance interface, shown in Figure 4-1, to communicate with them over the Internet.

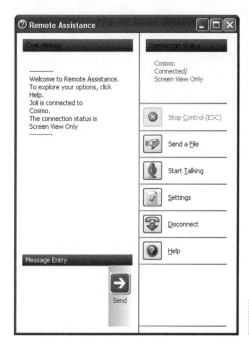

FIGURE 4-1 The Remote Assistance interface offers lots of options.

Here's the step-by-step instructions for getting remote assistance from a Windows Messenger buddy:

1. Click Start | Help And Support.

2. Under Ask For Assistance, choose Invite A Friend To Connect To Your Computer With Remote Assistance, as shown in Figure 4-2.

3. In the Remote Assistance window, in the right pane, select Invite Someone To Help You.

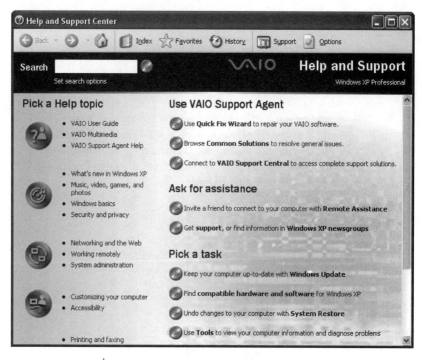

FIGURE 4-2　Invite a friend to help you

4. Remote Assistance will start, and you'll be given the option to choose a contact from your buddy list in Windows Messenger or to type in an e-mail address of any of your contacts, as shown in Figure 4-3. In this example, choose a Windows Messenger buddy who is online. To do so, you double-click the user to invite.

5. Wait while the user is invited. The user will have to accept the invitation. (You'll learn how to give remote assistance in the next section.) Once the user has accepted your invitation, click Yes when prompted to allow this person to view your screen and chat with you. If you choose No, the session will end.

6. To use a microphone in your conversations, click Start Talking.

7. Type your message in the Message Entry area and click Send.

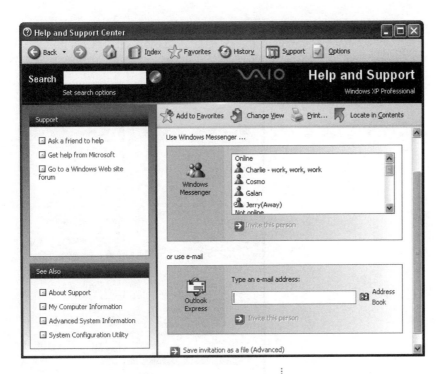

FIGURE 4-3 Choose a buddy to invite to help you

8. If and when your assistant wants to take control of your computer, they'll ask. (Again, you'll learn how to give assistance in the next section.) If you want to give control of the computer to your assistant, click Yes when prompted, as shown in Figure 4-4.

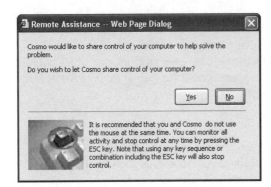

FIGURE 4-4 Giving up control using Remote Assistance

9. Your assistant can now control your computer screen and computer by moving their mouse. Figure 4-5 shows what the Remote Assistance interface looks like.

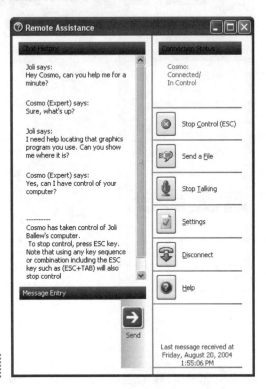

FIGURE 4-5 Control has been granted.

10. When you are finished with the Remote Assistance session, click Disconnect.

If you don't have your desired assistant on your Windows Messenger buddy list, you can send an invitation to any contact via e-mail. Once they've accepted, they'll use the code that's generated to make a secure connection to you. This means you can get remote assistance from anyone who's willing to help. Here are the step-by-step instructions for getting Remote Assistance from an e-mail contact:

1. Click Start | Help And Support.

2. Under Ask For Assistance, choose Invite A Friend To Connect To Your Computer With Remote Assistance, as shown earlier in Figure 4-2.

3. In the Remote Assistance window, in the right pane, select Invite Someone To Help You.

4. Remote Assistance will start, and you'll be given the option to choose a contact from your buddy list in Windows Messenger or to enter an e-mail address of any of your contacts. In this example, type in an e-mail address and then click Invite This Person, similar to what is shown in Figure 4-6.

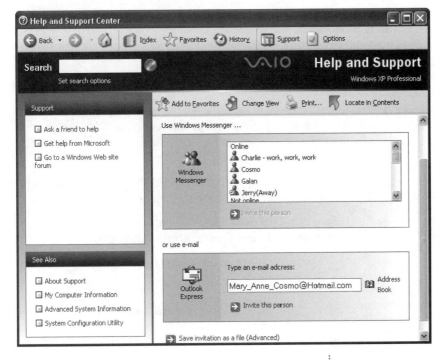

FIGURE 4-6 Invite a contact via e-mail

5. In the Remote Assistance—E-Mail An Invitation window, type a message and click Continue.

6. Set the expiration time for the invitation, check Require The Recipient To Use A Password, and type and confirm the password. Convey the password to the assistant, either by phone or in a separate e-mail. Click Send Invitation.

You may want to print these steps out for people who want to ask you for remote assistance.

7. After the recipient views the invitation, click Yes to let that person chat with you and view your computer screen. The remote assistance will continue as detailed in the previous example.

↘ Are You the Expert? Giving Remote Assistance

Giving remote assistance is almost as easy as getting it, except you have to know the answers!

If you are the one being asked to give assistance to a colleague, friend, or family member, you will receive the invitation to help in one of two ways: via a pop-up box from the Windows Messenger icon in your System Tray, or in the form of an e-mail in your Inbox.

If you're asked to give assistance from Windows Messenger:

1. A notification box will appear at the bottom-right part of the screen. Click this once to open the notification box. Next, click Accept to start the remote assistance session. The Windows Messenger interface will open automatically.

2. Wait while the person on the other end clicks Yes to let you chat with them, and then either of you can begin typing.

3. To take control of the other person's computer, first inform them of what you'd like to do, and then click Take Control.

4. You now have access to the user's computer and can show them how to solve their problem.

If you're asked to give assistance via an e-mail invitation:

1. Open the attachment; its file type is *.MsRcIncident. A sample of such is shown in Figure 4-7.

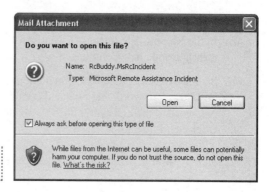

FIGURE 4-7 This is what the attachment will look like prior to opening it.

2. When prompted in the Remote Assistance dialog box, type the password received from the person asking for help.

3. Click Yes to connect.

➡ Preventing Remote Control of Your Computer

If you aren't using or planning to use Remote Assistance, disable it.

Spammers, virus writers, and the other evil-doers of the world are always thinking of new ways to gain access to your computer. It won't be long before gaining access using Remote Assistance scams become part of their ploy. Since you can never be too careful, it's generally a good idea to disable Remote Assistance until you need it. You can always turn it back on.

To prevent someone from taking control of your computer with a scam, and to prevent others from taking control of the computer using Remote Access:

1. Click Start | Control Panel.

2. Open System.

3. On the Remote tab, under Remote Assistance, select Advanced.

4. From the Remote Assistance Settings dialog box, uncheck Allow This Computer To Be Controlled Remotely, as shown in Figure 4-8.

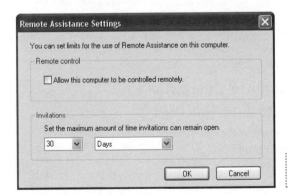

FIGURE 4-8 Do not let your computer be controlled remotely

ACCESS YOUR DESKTOP REMOTELY

Remote Desktop allows you to access your computer (or someone else's) remotely. In a common scenario, you leave your computer on at work, and when you get home, you access it from your own home office. It's just like sitting in front of it, including having access to all network resources, connected hardware such as printers, and all files stored on the computer's hard drive. Remote Desktop is secure too. When you leave your computer at work, you can lock it, so that only you can access it using CTRL-ALT-DEL.

To use Remote Desktop, you'll need the following:

- A remote computer (often an office computer) running Windows XP *Professional*, which is connected to the Internet or a local area connection.
- The remote computer must be configured to accept remote connections. (In other words, you have to configure your work computer for remote access before you leave work, and the work computer has to be left on and connected to the network. See the next section for more details.)
- A local computer (often the home computer or a work laptop you lug home with you) with access to that network. Connections can be made via the Internet, a LAN, or a virtual private network.
- The local computer must have Remote Desktop Connection configured.
- The local computer must have access to the LAN or the computer being accessed remotely.
- Users who will access the remote computer must have accounts and passwords on that computer. If you need more assistance on configuring accounts and passwords, refer to the Help and Support Center in Windows XP Professional.

Set Up the Remote Computer to Accept Remote Connections

Before you can connect to another computer remotely, it must be configured to accept the connection.

The remote computer is usually the office computer, often referred to as the *host* computer. Before a remote connection can be made to the host, certain criteria must be met and specific items have to be configured, as described in this section.

First, you must verify that Remote Desktop is enabled on the computer you wish to connect to:

1. Click Start | Control Panel.

2. If you're in Category view, open Performance And Maintenance. Select System.

3. In the System Properties dialog box, click the Remote tab.

4. Verify that Allow Remote Assistance Invitations To Be Sent From This Computer is checked, as shown in Figure 4-9. If a warning box appears, read it and click OK. Click Apply in the System Properties dialog box.

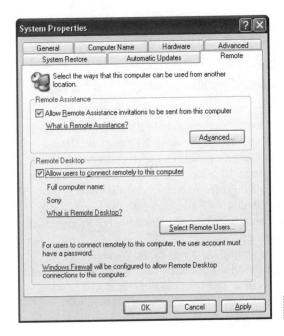

FIGURE 4-9 Enable Remote Desktop

Once you've enabled Remote Desktop, you must decide who you want to be able to access your computer.

5. On the Remote tab of the System Properties dialog box, click Select Remote Users. In the Remote Desktop Users dialog box, click Add.

6. Type a username for a person who has an account on this computer, and click Check Names. The result is shown in Figure 4-10. Click OK.

7. Click OK two more times to apply your selections.

With the remote (host) computer configured, you're ready to configure the computer that will be used to connect to it.

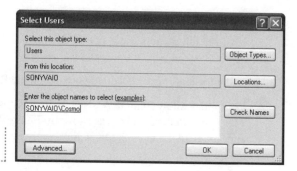

FIGURE 4-10 Add the users who can connect remotely

↘ Configure the Local Computer and Make the Connection

Before connecting to a remote computer, certain criteria have to be met on the local one.

To configure a computer to connect remotely to the host, the proper software must be installed. If you have a Windows XP computer (Home or Professional) with the latest service packs, you're ready to go. (And yes, that means Remote Desktop will work if the home PC has XP Home installed and the work PC has XP Professional installed.) If you have an operating system other than Windows XP (Windows 95 and later), you'll have to install the appropriate software from the Windows XP Professional CD-ROM onto that computer first.

Installing the software is simple. Just pop in the Windows XP Professional CD-ROM, click Perform Additional Tasks, and then click Set Up A Remote Desktop Connection. The wizard automatically installs the software and walks you though any additional steps.

Once the required software is available and installed, you simply make the connection:

FIGURE 4-11 Choose the computer you wish to connect to

1. From the local computer (which is also referred to as the *client* computer), click Start | Programs | Accessories | Communications | Remote Desktop Connection.

2. In the Remote Desktop Connection dialog box, type the name of the computer to connect to, as shown in Figure 4-11. Click Connect.

3. In the Log On To Windows dialog box, type the appropriate username and password. If the username and password do not exist on the host computer, or are not configured as a remote user, the login will fail. Click OK.

4. If another person is logged on to that computer, you'll be prompted to automatically log them off. Click Yes.

5. Once logged in, the user will have the option to close or restore the Remote Desktop window. Restoring the window causes the user to see a screen similar to the one shown in Figure 4-12, although their background and desktop may differ from what's shown here. The user can then access the computer under their account.

FIGURE 4-12 Make the connection

6. To end the session, simply click the Close button (X) at the top-right corner of the window.

↘ Get the Most Out of Remote Desktop

Remote Desktop can be tweaked to offer better performance.

In addition to connecting and accessing a remote computer locally, you can use the Remote Desktop configuration advanced options to help you get more from your connection.

To access the advanced options and configure how your connection will look and respond:

1. From the local (client) computer, click Start | Programs | Accessories | Communications | Remote Desktop Connection.

2. In the Remote Desktop Connection dialog box, shown earlier in Figure 4-11, click Options. The dialog box will expand, offering additional options, as shown in Figure 4-13.

FIGURE 4-13 Configure advanced options

There are five tabs available for setting advanced options: General, Display, Local Resources, Programs, and Experience. Each offers ways to personalize your connection to the remote computer.

On the General tab, you can configure the following items for automatic logon to a remote computer:

- **Computer** The name of the computer you'll log on to
- **User Name** The username

- **Password** The user's password

- **Domain** The domain, if applicable

- **Save My Password** Check to save the password

With the required information added, the user can log on automatically without having to type the information each time. The settings configured for this tab and others can also be saved to a file by using the Save As command. Click the Open button if you want to select a particular saved configuration, if multiple users have saved settings.

On the Display tab, you can configure how the remote desktop connection will look:

- **Remote Desktop Size** You can configure how large the remote connection's window will be.

- **Colors** You can configure how many colors to use when connected. More colors means a longer wait.

- **Display The Connection Bar When In Full Screen Mode** Lets you view the connection status (if you're connected, you'll see a bar across the top with the computer's name).

On the Local Resources tab, you can configure how you want sound, keyboard, and local devices to act:

- **Remote Computer Sound** You can choose to hear the remote computer's sounds, not play the sounds, or leave the sounds at the remote computer.

- **Keyboard** You can choose to have Windows key combinations like ALT-TAB active only when the remote computer's window is in full-screen mode, or have them always applied to the local computer or the remote one.

- **Local Devices** You can choose what local devices are active while logged on to the remote computer, including disk drives, printers, and serial ports. Figure 4-14 shows the defaults.

On the Programs tab, you can configure a program to start automatically each time you connect, by typing in the program path and the filename. The path is defined by a drive letter followed by a colon, a backslash, and the name of the folder and subfolder that contains the file or folder to open. An example could be C:\Program Files\Outlook Express.

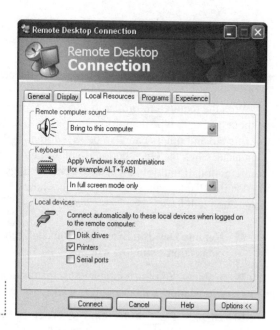

FIGURE 4-14 The default settings are usually best.

The last tab is the Experience tab, on which you can choose the connection speed to optimize performance as well as some display options:

- **Choose Your Connection Speed To Optimize Performance** Your choices are Modem (28.8), Modem (56.6), Broadband (128 Kbps – 1.5 Mbps), LAN (10 Mbps or higher), or Custom.

- **Desktop Background** Shows the remote computer's desktop background. By default, this is not selected.

- **Show Contents Of Windows While Dragging** Shows contents when folders are moved. By default, this is not selected.

- **Menu And Window Animation** Shows configured menus and window animations for the remote computer. By default, this is not selected.

- **Themes** Shows themes configured for the remote computer. By default, this is selected, but for better performance, it can be deselected.

- **Bitmap Caching** Places commonly used bitmaps, like the pictures used for My Documents, the Start menu, and similar items, in a file on the local computer. This improves performance because the information does not have to be continually sent over the lines.

For the most part, the defaults here are fine. Keep in mind, though, the more data that has to go from the remote computer to the local one, the slower performance will be.

CONNECT TO ANOTHER COMPUTER USING NETMEETING

Now that you can connect to your *own* work computer from home, let's look at ways to connect with *other people at other computers*. NetMeeting is an old standby for communicating over the Internet and phone lines, and was one of the earliest conferencing applications created by Microsoft. Communications with NetMeeting include chatting in real time, using web cams and/or microphones for video and voice communications, using an electronic whiteboard, and even sharing programs. Users can work collaboratively across the globe on graphics, documents, or proposals, without ever having to leave their office.

The good old days are gone, though; NetMeeting is no longer an application that is installed by default, and it is not an option in the All Programs menu. However, if you know the trick, you can install and use it in both Windows XP Home and Windows XP Professional. Doing so will create new and efficient ways to conference and communicate with friends, family, and colleagues over the Internet.

◥ Where Is NetMeeting?

You likely don't know where NetMeeting is, and if you look for it, you probably won't find it either.

If you've never used NetMeeting in Windows XP, I bet you don't know where it is. Go ahead, look in All Programs, Accessories, or even Communications. You won't find it. Want to know the trick? You have to install it first (and you don't even need the Windows XP CD-ROM).

To install and run NetMeeting and make it available on your computer:

1. Click Start | Run and type **conf**. Click OK.

2. In the NetMeeting dialog box, click Next to work through the wizard and install the program. If you've previously installed it, NetMeeting will start automatically. The NetMeeting interface is shown in Figure 4-15.

FIGURE 4-15　NetMeeting offers new ways to communicate.

3. As you work through the wizard, you'll be required to:

- Fill in the information for name, e-mail address, etc.

- Select Microsoft Internet Directory as the default.

- Select the connection speed.

- Choose whether or not to place a shortcut on the Desktop.

- Test and configure your microphone, if one is installed.

Connect to Others with NetMeeting

There are lots of ways to connect with others, including dialing directly into their computer, or connecting using an IP address, connecting via e-mail address, or even by computer name.

Once NetMeeting is installed on both computers that will be used for communicating, you start it by clicking Start | Run and typing **conf**. Once started, you can make a connection in a number of ways. You can type in an e-mail address, a phone number, an IP address, or a computer name. Each are similar, and with an understanding of how to make a connection and communicate on the most basic level, the rest will fall into place easily. Let's look first at the easiest way to connect, using a LAN.

To connect over a LAN:

1. Click Start | Run and type **conf**. Click OK. NetMeeting will start.

2. To place a call, either click Call | New Call or click the telephone icon on the interface.

3. In the Place A Call dialog box, shown in Figure 4-16, type the name of the computer to call. Click Call.

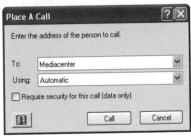

FIGURE 4-16 Type the computer name to connect over a LAN

 If you aren't sure of the name of the computer, you have several options. You can open My Network Places, and from the Network Tasks pane, select View Workgroup Computers; or, you can click Start | Search, use the Other Search Options, and click Computers Or People. There you can search for computers on the network.

4. A ringing sound will occur on the recipient's computer; if they accept the invitation to open NetMeeting, you'll be connected. Once connected, you'll see something similar to what's shown in Figure 4-17.

5. The four ways to communicate are offered as icons at the bottom of the interface (from left to right): Share Program, Chat, Whiteboard, Transfer Files. Click any icon to use that method. Figure 4-18 shows a chat in progress.

FIGURE 4-17 NetMeeting in a call

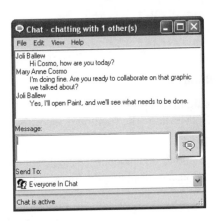

FIGURE 4-18 Chatting in NetMeeting

As mentioned previously, you can initiate a conversation in a number of ways. To connect by dialing a phone number, the other computer must first be set up to receive dialed calls to it, a rather complicated process that is usually done by a network administrator (or, in many homes, by a teenager). However, once the computer is correctly configured, connecting is as simple as dialing the telephone number. It's also possible to connect using an e-mail address. If you have the other person's e-mail address, though, Windows Messenger may be an easier alternative, and is generally the preferred method.

There's quite a bit of help regarding the setup process to receive dialed calls in XP's Help and Support Center.

Use Group Policy to Secure NetMeeting

If you're going to use NetMeeting for communicating and conferencing, make sure it's secure.

As with other Microsoft applications, Group Policy offers ways to configure and secure NetMeeting. If you're going to be using NetMeeting as a communication and conferencing tool, looking over the options is a good idea. Using Group Policy requires that you have Windows XP Professional, though; you won't be able to do this in Windows XP Home Edition.

If you need help starting the Group Policy Editor or want to read an overview of it, refer to Chapter 1.

To open the Group Policy Editor and locate and configure NetMeeting options:

1. Click Start | Run and type **gpedit.msc**.
2. Expand the following: User Configuration | Administrative Tools | Windows Components. Select NetMeeting. The resulting window is shown in Figure 4-19.
3. To configure application-sharing options, double-click the Application Sharing folder in the right pane. Consider disabling the following for higher security:

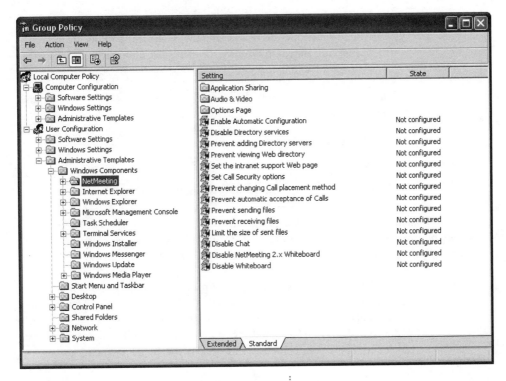

FIGURE 4-19 The NetMeeting security options

- Prevent Desktop Sharing

- Prevent Sharing Command Prompts

- Prevent Control

4. To configure audio and video options, open the Audio & Video folder. Consider disabling the following for higher security:

- Limit The Bandwidth Of Audio And Video

- Prevent Receiving Video

5. To configure general options for NetMeeting, open the Options Page folder. Consider disabling the following for higher security (regarding the users that use NetMeeting at your computer):

- Hide The Security Page

- Hide The Video Page

6. There are also some security options listed as stand-alone options, which can be viewed by opening the NetMeeting folder. Those options are shown in Figure 4-19. Consider configuring the following for higher security:

- Prevent Automatic Acceptance Of Calls

- Prevent Receiving Files

- Limit The Size Of Sent Files

- Disable Chat

7. Close the Group Policy Editor when finished.

 Be careful to remember what you've changed just in case you need to revert back later! NetMeeting may be needed to receive files later, or to view videos. Make sure you know how to make the required changes in the Group Policy Editor quickly if this happens.

So that's about it for working (and playing) remotely using Windows XP's included applications. And, ending on a secure note makes moving into the next chapter an easy transition. Chapter 5 explores the newest addition to Windows XP, Service Pack 2. Using SP2's options, you'll be able to further tweak and secure your computer, in ways previously unattainable.

CHAPTER 5
SAFETY FIRST: SERVICE PACK 2

Microsoft's latest upgrade to Windows XP is called Service Pack 2. Its main purpose is to keep your computer and your personal privacy as secure as humanly and technologically possible. It offers security enhancements to Internet Explorer and Outlook Express, as well as an enhanced, automatic firewall (a little more about this later) that blocks pop-up ads and helps guard against Internet threats like viruses and spyware. Service Pack 2 has a new Security Center in Control Panel, and a new applet for setting up a wireless network. If for some reason you haven't yet downloaded, obtained, or installed Service Pack 2, it's time to do so. Once installed, you can safely join your friends, family, and coworkers on the Internet without worrying about the latest security threats.

HOW TO GET SERVICE PACK 2

There are multiple ways to obtain Service Pack 2, including the easiest, which is to let the update download automatically through Windows XP's Automatic Updates feature. It's a huge file, a whopping 272MB, so it's configured such that the download will pick up where it left off if you get disconnected or log off. This is a great way to get the update if you have an "always on" connection to the Internet.

Besides automatic updates, though, which won't work for those who aren't online very often or who have a dial-up connection, there are other options. SP2 also can be obtained from Microsoft's Windows Update web site, it can be ordered on a CD-ROM and shipped to your home, or it can be installed by a technician at your local computer store.

In this section, you'll learn the best way to get SP2 no matter what kind of setup you have. If you're on dial-up, the CD-ROM is probably the best option for you. You won't have to worry about being online long enough to get it, or keep track of how much of it you've received, or if it will install properly once it's on your hard drive. If you're not online very often, perhaps because your computer is a laptop, or because you just don't use the computer that much, purchasing the CD is a good option too. However, there are other options besides paying for the CD.

Anyone with a valid and licensed copy of Windows XP can go to the Windows Update web site and manually download SP2. If you have the time, this is a good option. You can also choose any other updates that you'd like to install, such as updated drivers or other optional updates.

A final option is to take your computer to a computer store and let a technician install it. It won't be free, but at least you'll know it'll be done correctly! Let's look at all of these options in detail.

If you don't know if you have SP2 or not, right-click My Computer and check the General tab. It will be noted in the information there.

◥ Wait for Automatic Updates or Get the Update Manually

The easiest way to get Service Pack 2 is through Automatic Updates.

To obtain Service Pack 2 through Automatic Updates, you must have Automatic Updates enabled. You also have to leave your computer on and connected to the Internet for a substantial period of time so that the download can occur. If you turn off your computer or disconnect from the Internet, the download will pick up where it left off the next time you connect. This is all done behind the scenes without any inconvenience to you. You won't even notice it downloading if you have broadband; you may notice a slowdown when the update is downloading over a dial-up connection.

 *Free download accelerators are available, including DAP7, Download Accelerator Plus (**http://www.speedbit.com**). This application allows you to download files up to 300 times faster than without it, among other features.*

Once the download has finished, you'll be prompted that new updates are ready to install. A small balloon will appear, as shown in Figure 5-1. Simply click to install the update.

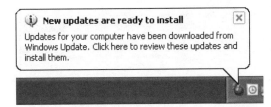

FIGURE 5-1 This balloon will appear when the update is ready to install.

To verify that Automatic Updates is enabled:

1. Right-click My Computer and choose Properties.

2. Click the Automatic Updates tab.

3. Verify that Automatic Updates is enabled.

If you don't want to wait for the update to download, if you have a slow connection, or if you have a dial-up connection to the Internet and don't want to get the update using this method, order the CD-ROM from **http://www.microsoft.com/windowsxp/downloads/**. Select Windows XP Service Pack 2 and follow the links.

If you don't want to pay to have the CD-ROM shipped to you, or if you aren't online long enough to get Service Pack 2 via Automatic Updates, you can log on to the Windows Update web site and manually obtain the update. If you're a dial-up user, manually downloading the update from the Windows Update web site gives you a chance to log on and control when the download occurs. If you wait for Windows Update, it will come piecemeal over a longer period of time. The Windows Update web site can be accessed by clicking Start | All Programs | Windows Update. The instructions are clear for downloading; simply wait while your system is scanned, and then choose Express Install, as shown in Figure 5-2.

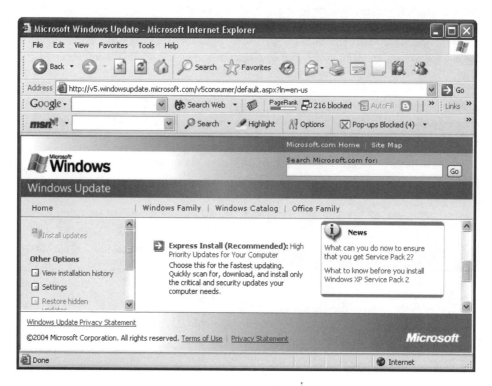

FIGURE 5-2 SP2 can be obtained manually from Windows Update.

⬎ Get SP2 at Your Local Computer Store

Have someone else do the work for you, but it will help to do a little preparation beforehand.

If you don't want to install Service Pack 2 yourself, if you have a dial-up connection, or if you have a high-speed connection but aren't online very much because your computer isn't turned on all the time, take your computer to your local computer store for the upgrade.

Most computer stores offer technical support. Most of the time, the technicians repair nonworking computers, add RAM, replace hard drives, and add ports. However, most now also perform software upgrades, including installing Service Pack 2. Unfortunately, the technicians also take time out to tell you that you need to purchase a few other items, namely pop-up stopper software, system tune-ups, and additional hardware. Much of the time you don't need it, so be careful.

Before taking your computer in to your local computer store, do the following to guarantee a smooth installation and to avoid unnecessary "recommendations" by the computer technician:

- Make sure your antivirus software is up to date.

- Run Disk Cleanup and Disk Defragmenter to make sure your computer is not storing unnecessary or fragmented files.

- Use msconfig (click Start | Run) to disable programs you don't need.

- Visit the web site of your computer manufacturer and get any driver or software updates offered.

- Make a complete backup of your data.

The object is to locate and solve potential problems before the technician finds them. What you can perform on your own could cost upwards of $200 at the store. Once the technician finishes, have them boot the computer for you before you head home; once booted, verify that SP2 has been installed:

1. Right-click My Computer and choose Properties.

2. On the General tab, verify that SP2 is listed, as shown in Figure 5-3.

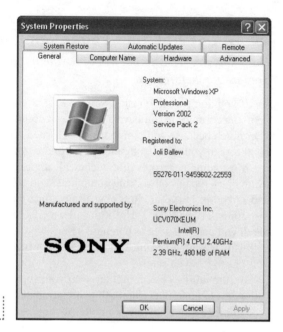

FIGURE 5-3 Checking that SP2 is installed

INTERNET SECURITY

Service Pack 2 applies lots of changes to both Internet Explorer and Outlook Express regarding security and privacy. However, many of these changes were created with application developers and corporate administrators in mind, not the average power user. For the most part, what you'll be interested in is how to get applications to work the way they did *before* SP2 was installed. For instance, you'll be unable to open attachments in Outlook Express until you reconfigure some settings, and you might have trouble downloading files in Internet Explorer until you enable the Automatic Prompting For File Downloads option in Security Settings. Thus, this section touches on some of the new features while focusing on managing the new settings.

Popping Pop-Ups

The Pop-Up Blocker is nice, but you may want to tweak it a bit.

There are a few new features worth noting in Internet Explorer. One is the new Pop-Up Blocker. Blocking pop-ups protects you from malicious web sites that either reset your home page or, worse, install a program or obtain information about you from your computer unwillingly. Having a pop-up blocker is simply a nice feature, too, because it blocks unwanted ads.

Unfortunately, the new Pop-Up Blocker can also cause problems. Many web sites use pop-up dialog boxes to allow you to log in, input registration information, print receipts, or display videos or other information. If you visit such a web site, you can make an exception for that web site and still keep the Pop-Up Blocker enabled.

By default, the Pop-Up Blocker is enabled. You can disable it easily, or tweak it to disable it for specific web sites:

1. To disable the Pop-Up Blocker completely, in Internet Explorer, select Tools | Internet Options and click the Privacy tab. Uncheck Block Pop-Ups, as shown in Figure 5-4. Click OK.

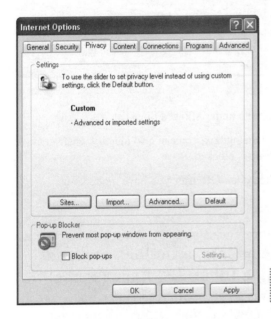

FIGURE 5-4 You can disable the Pop-Up Blocker if you don't like it or if you use another program.

2. If you have not disabled the Pop-Up Blocker but simply want to tweak it to allow specific sites to offer pop-ups, in Internet Explorer, click Tools | Internet Options and then click the Privacy tab.

3. Under Pop-Up Blocker, click Settings to open the Pop-Up Blocker Settings dialog box, shown in Figure 5-5.

4. Type or paste in the Address Of Web Site To Allow list box the URL of the web site you want to allow pop-ups for. (If you type it, as you start to type, autocomplete will offer previously viewed sites.)

FIGURE 5-5 Add allowed sites when pop-ups are warranted

5. Click Add to add the site to the Allowed Sites list.

6. At the bottom of the dialog box, you can also identify what should happen when a pop-up is blocked.

7. Click Close and then click OK after you have made your configurations.

➥ Opening Attachments in Outlook Express (and Confronting Other SP2 Annoyances)

There are plenty of annoyances about SP2, especially its reversal of your personal Outlook Express security settings to their defaults.

SP2 also changes default settings in Outlook Express. While these changes produce a more secure computer, they reduce functionality for almost all users. The first problem with the new settings is that attachments can no longer be opened. You'll see the paper clip that indicates an attachment was sent with the message, but it will be grayed out. Attachments are a big part of productivity for businesses and home users alike, and are an integral part of e-mailing. The second problem with the new settings it that all HTML content in e-mails is blocked, which also reduces functionality. Again, I must stress that this produces a more secure computer … but certainly not a more usable one.

If you want to open attachments, you need to tweak a single setting:

1. In Outlook Express, click Tools | Options.

2. Click the Security tab, shown in Figure 5-6.

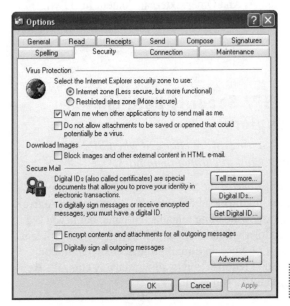

FIGURE 5-6 Allow attachments in Outlook Express

3. Uncheck Do Not Allow Attachments To Be Saved Or Opened That Could Potentially Be A Virus.

4. If the Restricted Sites Zone (More Secure) radio button is selected, that will also limit your functionality. If you have third-party virus protection installed, choosing this radio button is likely unnecessary. Therefore, select the Internet Zone (Less Secure, But More Functional) radio button. Click OK.

The second item you may want to tweak involves HTML content in e-mails. When you receive e-mail from web sites and online retailers, they may contain tiny, invisible images called *web bugs*. These bugs can be used to identify you online and track your surfing habits. Because this is a threat, SP2 blocks these by default. However, if you often get e-mail that contains HTML content including pictures, the same content that the bugs are created with, you won't get the pictures you're used to. Your e-mail will be pretty bland. To revert to earlier days and allow HTML content to open automatically in e-mails:

1. In Outlook Express, click Tools | Options.

2. Click the Security tab.

3. Uncheck Block Images And Other External Content In HTML E-Mail.

4. Click OK.

↘ Restore Pre-SP2 Security Settings in Internet Explorer

Many Internet Explorer settings were changed when SP2 was installed, and you might want to change them back.

You may want to change two of the SP2 Internet Explorer settings in particular. One has to do with downloading programs, another with ActiveX controls. For the most part, downloading remains the same, but if you use advanced programs or run Internet macros, you'll likely encounter problems. Problems can also occur if you use an e-mail program like Trillian or Hotmail, or anything else that requires you to allow ActiveX controls. By default, ActiveX controls are blocked in SP2.

 ActiveX controls are similar to Java applets, but are potentially more harmful. They can cause damage to your computer.

When you want to download a file or program from the Internet, you're usually prompted with a download box that asks you whether you're sure that you want to download it and, if so, where to save it. The reason that you are asked to agree before files or programs are downloaded to your computer is to help you protect the computer from malicious programs. Unfortunately, when running Internet macros and similar programs, Internet Explorer completely blocks the option to download files when you don't want it to. If you're ever prompted with a notice that a file you wanted to download was blocked, you'll need to tweak a setting in Internet Explorer to allow it:

1. Open Internet Explorer and click Tools | Internet Options.

2. Click the Security tab, click the Internet icon, and then click Custom Level.

3. In the Security Settings dialog box, scroll down to Downloads and, under Automatic Prompting For File Downloads, click Enable, as shown in Figure 5-7.

4. Click OK, and click OK again to close the dialog boxes.

If you ever get a prompt that says "Internet Explorer has restricted this file from showing ActiveX content that could access your computer. Click here for options" you'll need to enable ActiveX controls:

1. In Internet Explorer, click Tools | Internet Options and then click the Advanced tab.

2. Scroll down to Security.

3. Check Allow Active Content To Run In Files On My Computer.

4. Click OK.

FIGURE 5-7 Change default security settings when problems with downloads occur

NEW CONTROL PANEL APPLETS

The first thing you'll likely notice about SP2 are the three new Control Panel applets:

- ■ **Windows Firewall**   Lets you view and change firewall settings.

- ■ **Security Center**   Offers a place to quickly view the security settings, in particular to see if the firewall, Automatic Updates, and virus protection are enabled. You can also manage Internet security options.

- ■ **Wireless Network Setup Wizard**   Lets you easily set up your wireless network after you've purchased and installed the hardware.

↘ Configure Windows Firewall

Windows Firewall helps you stay secure no matter where you go on the Internet.

When Service Pack 2 is first installed, Windows Firewall is turned on by default. A *firewall* is software that helps keep your computer secure by restricting what comes into the computer from a local network or the Internet. What can come in are viruses, worms, spyware, and even malicious programs.

Windows Firewall is pretty secure, and the highest level of protection is enabled. Windows Firewall won't even let you receive files from people that you instant message with without your express permission. If you want to receive the file, you have to tell the firewall you want to create an *exception*. An exception is a special exclusion that you create when prompted. You'll be prompted if need be; however, you may never be prompted if you engage in safe surfing, are not part of a network, or never use Remote Assistance or Remote Desktop (among other things).

 If you have a third-party firewall program installed, turn off SP2's Windows Firewall.

To see what settings are configured by default, turn off Windows Firewall, create exceptions manually, or configure advanced firewall properties:

1. Open Control Panel and then Windows Firewall.

2. Click the General tab, shown in Figure 5-8. Here, you can turn off Windows Firewall or choose to not allow exceptions. You should turn off Windows Firewall if you have another firewall program running, and disallow exceptions if you are using your computer in a public place, such as an airport.

FIGURE 5-8 By default, Windows Firewall is turned on.

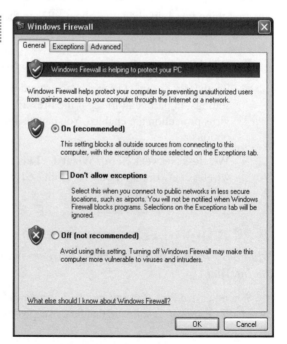

3. Click the Exceptions tab. You don't have to add exceptions manually if you don't want to; if you ever need a program (such as Remote Desktop or Remote Assistance), you'll be prompted to create an exception then. However, if you do want to add an exception manually, select Add Program offered under this tab and select the program from the list provided.

4. Click the Advanced tab. Here, you can view what is protected, which generally includes your Internet connection and network connections. The defaults are almost always fine and should not be changed. You can also create a Security log to see successful connections and dropped packets. When e-mail is sent across the Internet, it's broken up into *packets* instead of being sent in one piece. When packets are dropped by the firewall, they do not make it to your computer.

5. Click OK to accept the changes you've made or Cancel to use the existing settings when finished.

➘ Rely on the Security Center

The Security Center gives you a quick overview of your security settings.

The Security Center is also located in Control Panel. There isn't much you can do with it, though; it's really just a place to see if your protection settings are configured the way Microsoft recommends. If you have a third-party firewall, if your computer is configured to get automatic updates manually, or if you don't use virus protection and don't want to be alerted about these issues, you will want to turn off the notification for those features.

Figure 5-9 shows a healthy system report from the Security Center. If you have any of these configured as Off, you'll also want to turn off notification for them (that is, unless you enjoy being notified about your settings all of the time).

To turn off notification:

1. Open Control Panel and Security Center.

2. In the Resources area, click Change The Way Security Center Alerts Me.

3. Uncheck the items desired, and click OK.

4. Close the Security Center.

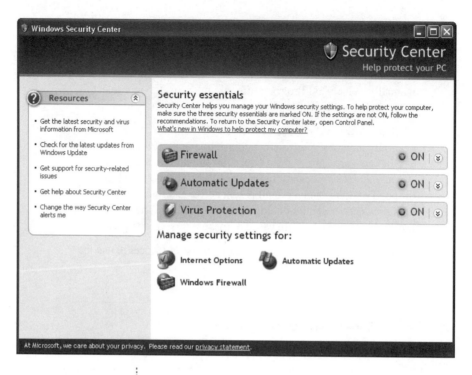

FIGURE 5-9 A healthy system report

↘ Use the Wireless Network Setup Wizard

When you're ready to go wireless, use this wizard.

The Wireless Network Setup Wizard is another new feature offered by Service Pack 2. You can use this wizard after you've purchased and installed the wireless hardware required for your computers, as well as the associated wireless access point(s). Access points are what allow the information to be transmitted wirelessly, and are a required part of the wireless network. These can also be routers.

While working through the wizard, you'll have only a few decisions to make, but to do so you'll need a brief understanding of the technology behind the network you want to create. As a primer, prior to running the wizard, make sure you've answered these questions:

■ What will your new wireless network be named?

■ Is all of the hardware installed, as well as any drivers and software that came with it?

■ Do you know what a network key is? Do you have your own network key or will you let the wizard assign one automatically? (Automatically is generally best.)

■ Are your devices WPA (Wi-Fi Protected Access) compatible? WPA is a stronger encryption, but not all devices are compatible at this time.

■ Do you have a USB flash drive for storing the network settings so they can be used to set up other computers? If not, you can print the settings and store them in a safe location.

■ If you have a wireless printer, have all software and drivers been installed?

Once you can answer these questions, you'll be ready to run the wizard. The wizard is simple to use, and self-explanatory. Figure 5-10 shows the option to save the settings to a USB flash drive.

FIGURE 5-10 The Wireless Network Setup Wizard offers an easy way to save network settings.

Now that you've worked with SP2, configured the firewall, and changed the SP2 default settings of Internet Explorer and Outlook Express so that they run as you prefer, it's time to break for a little fun. In the next chapter, I'll discuss gaming, specifically how to build a better PC with additional hardware, and how to get better performance by tweaking the operating system settings. By using hardware profiles, for instance, you can disable everything that isn't needed to play games in order to get the best gaming performance possible.

CHAPTER 6
STAYING IN THE GAME

Windows XP is generally a good out-of-the-box system for gamers. For the most part, any new midrange or better computer that ships with XP preinstalled is pretty well equipped for gaming. Of course, you can always buy a better machine that is optimized for gaming. For example, if you can afford it, Alienware offers the best gaming computers around. However, if you can't afford a top-of-the-line performance computer, there are ways to increase gaming performance with the one you currently own.

In this chapter, you'll first learn how to beef up your current system with hardware upgrades, such as RAM and video or sound cards. Next, you'll learn a few software tricks, like how to create a gaming hardware profile. Finally, you discover how Service Pack 2 affects your gaming experience. I'll also invite you to throw your own LAN party!

BUILD A BETTER PC

Better hardware, faster CPUs, more RAM, and ultimate gaming sound and video cards make for a better gaming experience. Even if you couldn't afford the most expensive computer on the market when you purchased your PC, you can almost certainly spice it up with a few hardware purchases. The best way, of course, is to add more RAM.

⬊ Beef Up Your System with RAM

RAM always increases performance.

RAM, or random access memory, is physical hardware inside the computer case. RAM holds data that the computer uses (or expects to use) for the next calculations. RAM is also used to store data temporarily, such as a file on its way to the printer, an open document that has not been saved, or a photo before and after editing. RAM stores instructions and data, and this data can be accessed many times faster than data stored on the hard disk. To acquire data from a hard disk, the disk must spin, the data must be found, and then the data must be accessed. If the necessary data is stored in RAM, it's simply pulled immediately. No spinning or locating is required. Very simply, RAM stores the data that is needed and accessed often by a game.

Since data from RAM is accessed so much more quickly than data from a hard disk, the more RAM you have installed, the better. For gamers, this refers to RAM installed on the motherboard itself, as well as *onboard* RAM that comes with higher-end sound and video cards.

To find out what kind of RAM you need, whether you have the available slots on the motherboard, how much you can install, and how to purchase RAM online and from a reputable retailer, you can download and install Crucial Technology's Belarc Advisor. This program is a free application that tells you all you need to know to get the RAM you need:

1. Open your web browser and go to **http:// www.crucial.com**.

2. In the Product Search box, type **Belarc Advisor** and click Go. From the results, locate the link Where Can I Find The Belarc Advisor and click.

3. After locating the link to start the Belarc Advisor, click it to begin and choose to download the application. When prompted what to do, click Run. The dialog box is shown in Figure 6-1.

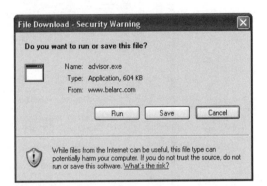

FIGURE 6-1 Crucial's Belarc Advisor gives you the information you need to choose the correct RAM for your machine.

4. When prompted again about the application, click Run. Click Install to automatically install the program. Wait while a profile of your computer's hardware is created.

5. The results will show in your web browser. Figure 6-2 shows an example. Write down the RAM type and size, and your computer's make and manufacturer. Click the Back button on your browser, and then search for the RAM required.

Installing RAM is often times as simple as opening the case and placing the RAM in the appropriate slot on the motherboard. Instructions come with the RAM you purchase, if you go with a reliable retailer. Unfortunately, installing RAM isn't always this easy, especially if the RAM is hidden underneath other components or if it's extremely small, as with a laptop. If you open the case and the old RAM doesn't appear to be easily accessible, you should take your computer and the new RAM to a service center.

In addition to problems associated with difficult-to-install RAM (and keep in mind, it usually *is* easy to install), you also have to follow the directions to the letter. For instance, you must always properly ground yourself before touching anything inside the case, because even a small shock to the motherboard can damage it. You also must hold and handle the RAM properly, so that you do not damage it either. If you do decide to install the RAM yourself, just make sure you read and follow all the directions.

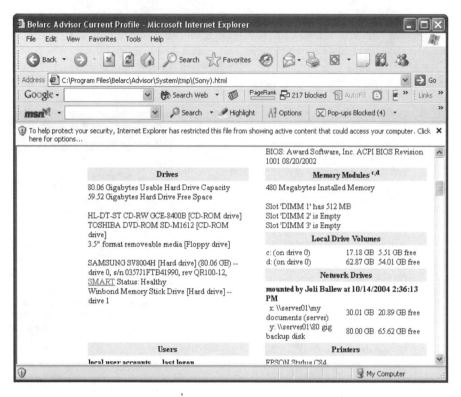

FIGURE 6-2 A sample report shows two open slots that can hold 512MB of DIMM 1 RAM each.

 The Belarc Advisor report also lists all installed applications' product keys, all installed and network printers, multimedia devices, virus protection, and software licenses and versions.

↘ Upgrade Sound and Video Cards

There's no better way to increase performance for sound and visual effect than to obtain and install the best cards possible.

If you want to increase game performance in ways other than by adding RAM, upgrading your sound and video cards is a great option. Higher-end sound and video cards aren't that expensive, and will greatly improve what you see and hear when playing. That's because higher-end models have their own onboard RAM and their own small processors. They actually do help the computer run better, especially when it comes to games.

To install either card, you simply turn off the computer, open the case, pull the old card (the sound card is the one located where the microphone plugs in, and the video card is the one located where the monitor plugs in) and replace it with a new one. Replace the cover and reboot. It's as simple as that.

While installing a new card is pretty easy, deciding what to purchase can be quite trying. Again, the Belarc Advisor noted in the last section can give you information about what you already have, or you can open the case and take a look for yourself. Figure 6-3 shows some basic information from the Advisor regarding the display adapter, the monitor, and multimedia audio devices.

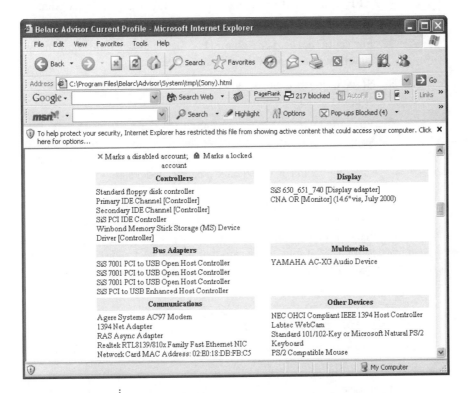

FIGURE 6-3 The Belarc Advisor offers information about multimedia hardware too.

So how do you go about deciding what card to buy? Well, your first consideration is cost. Sound cards run $30 and up, as do video cards. Cards can run over $200 or more for a good one. You get what you pay for, so spend as much as you're comfortable spending. You'll probably also want to purchase better speakers once the sound card is installed, and perhaps even a better monitor, so keep that in mind too.

However much you decide to spend, here's the absolute basics for what you should look for in a sound card and/or a video card:

- **Compatibility with Windows XP and your games**   If you have games already installed, look at their minimum requirements and make sure you get a card that's listed.

- **Properly tested and signed drivers**   Make sure the card's drivers have been tested by Microsoft and are on Microsoft's Hardware Compatibility List.

- **API support**   If you have games already installed, know what APIs you'll need, because you may need specific support.

- **For sound cards, 128+ channels**   Channels determine how many simultaneous sounds the card can handle at a time.

- **Stereo, quadraphonic, surround sound, and 3-D sound support**   Get as much as you can afford and desire.

- **For video cards, 128+ of onboard RAM and DirectX 9.0 support**   Onboard RAM allows data to be saved to the RAM on the card instead of the RAM on the motherboard, and DirectX 9.0 support guarantees you'll have a newer model card.

If you're really serious about gaming, you'll probably want to replace your video card at least once a year. As for audio, a good set of speakers can really enhance even a mediocre sound card. When shopping for speakers, at least go for a set of four, and a card that supports 4.1 audio or higher. It's been my experience that Klipsch offers the best audio available.

↘ Throw a LAN Party

There's nothing quite as fun as throwing a LAN party and playing games into the night with friends.

If you love games like Half-Life or Quake, and you have friends who like the same, you don't have to go online to play against each other—you can create your own network, connect your own computers, and annihilate each other while everyone sits in the same room, attic, or basement. Hearing your opponent actually groan when you kill him is certainly worth the time it takes to set it up!

If this is your first LAN party, to start, just invite three or four players. Each player has to have their own laptop or computer and a network interface card. You have to have room and support for it all, including the required electrical outlets, power strips, and desks and chairs. Once all of the computers are set up, connect them all to a hub or wirelessly to an access point.

Once everyone is physically connected, you need to get them all connected to the network. On each computer, run the Network Setup Wizard as follows:

1. Click Start | All Programs | Accessories | Communications | Network Setup Wizard.

2. Click Next, and click Next again to start the wizard.

3. Because you'll likely not be online while playing, click Other, and then click This Computer Belongs To A Network That Does Not Have An Internet Connection, as shown in Figure 6-4. Click Next.

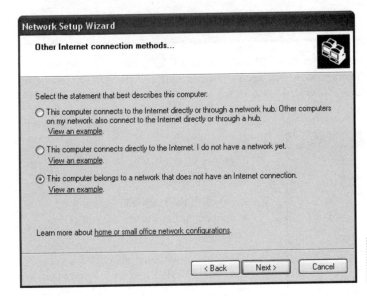

FIGURE 6-4 Setting up a network without an Internet connection is easiest.

4. For each computer, create a computer description using the player's name, and for the computer name, type the user's last name, as shown in Figure 6-5. All computer names on the network must be different from each other. Click Next.

5. For the workgroup name, type LAN PARTY. Click Next.

6. Click Next to complete the wizard and restart all computers. Have each computer join the LAN PARTY workgroup.

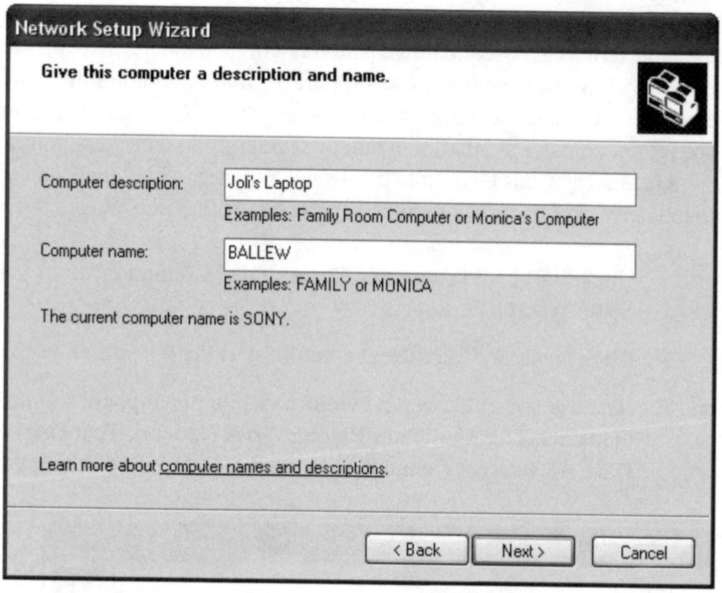

Network Setup Wizard

Give this computer a description and name.

Computer description: | Joli's Laptop

Examples: Family Room Computer or Monica's Computer

Computer name: | BALLEW

Examples: FAMILY or MONICA

The current computer name is SONY.

Learn more about computer names and descriptions.

< Back | Next > | Cancel

FIGURE 6-5 Personalize each computer

If any user has a static IP address, they'll have problems connecting. If that's the case, each will need to tweak their TCP/IP settings to obtain a DNS address automatically. These next steps are required only for those users:

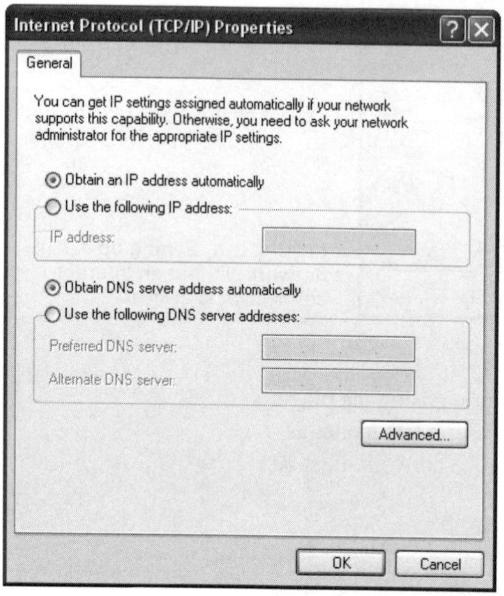

Internet Protocol (TCP/IP) Properties

General

You can get IP settings assigned automatically if your network supports this capability. Otherwise, you need to ask your network administrator for the appropriate IP settings.

◉ Obtain an IP address automatically
○ Use the following IP address:
IP address:

◉ Obtain DNS server address automatically
○ Use the following DNS server addresses:
Preferred DNS server:
Alternate DNS server:

Advanced...

OK | Cancel

FIGURE 6-6 IP information must be obtained automatically.

1. Click Start | Control Panel, and if in Category view, click Network And Internet Connections. Open Network Connections.

2. Right-click the LAN connection used to connect to the workgroup and select Properties.

3. Click the Networking tab, click Internet Protocol (TCP/IP), and click Properties.

4. On the General tab, click both Obtain An IP Address Automatically and Obtain DNS Server Address Automatically, as shown in Figure 6-6. Click OK, and click OK again to apply the settings.

5. Reboot the computer if prompted.

Finally, get gaming! Fire up the program and start the mayhem!

OPTIMIZE SYSTEM SETTINGS

Even if you have the best hardware in the world, if you have five gazillion programs or services running in the background, the CPU is going to bog down and games will not run effectively. If you're just in it for the game, you don't need your computer keeping track of updates or reporting errors while you're playing. You also shouldn't be using themes, and you may need a specific screen resolution configured for the games you want to play.

When so many changes and tweaks can be (or need to be) made when game playing, it's often best to create a gaming hardware profile. This profile will show as an option when booting. If you're booting the computer for game playing, boot using the resource-saving gaming profile, which should also be configured with the correct screen resolution; if you're booting the computer for word processing or art creation, use a regular profile and a screen resolution required for those programs.

6

◥ Create a Hardware Profile

You can create a hardware profile just for gaming, and disable unnecessary services and hardware.

In Chapter 2, you learned about some of the unnecessary services and applications that aren't needed when running XP. Handwriting services, the Indexing Service, Fast User Switching, and similar items use system resources, and can be disabled. Remember, the less your computer has to do, the better it will do what you ask of it. So, when creating a computer configuration for gaming, you'll continue in this vein, turning off anything that isn't needed and reserving computer power for your games. You'll save the configuration as a *gaming profile*, one you'll choose when you boot your computer.

Your gaming profile will be a bare-bones operating system; you'll turn off services such as Routing and Remote Access, ClipBook, Computer Browser, Error Reporting Service, etc. While these are certainly important in everyday computing, they aren't necessary when playing games. Turning off unnecessary services will increase the speed of your computer. You simply choose the profile when you want to play games.

To create a hardware profile for gaming:

1. Choose Start | Control Panel and choose System.

2. In the System Properties dialog box, click the Hardware tab.

3. Click Hardware Profiles.

FIGURE 6-7 Create a gaming profile

4. In the Hardware Profiles dialog box, click Copy.

5. Type **Gaming Profile** to name the profile. Click OK. Figure 6-7 shows the result.

6. For now, choose Wait Until I Select A Hardware Profile. Once you know both profiles are working and functional, you can change these options to always boot to the original profile after a few seconds, if one has not been selected yet.

7. Click OK, and click OK again.

8. Reboot to the new profile.

After rebooting to the new profile, you can tweak that profile to your heart's content. Work through Chapter 2 to learn how to disable unnecessary services and applications. Some additional services you can disable include

- Routing and Remote Access
- ClipBook
- COM+ System Application
- Computer Browser
- Help and Support
- Internet Connection Firewall/Internet Connection Sharing
- Net Logon
- Performance Logs and Alerts
- Remote Desktop Help Session Manager
- Remote Registry
- Removable Storage
- Secondary Logon
- Server
- Smart Card
- Smart Card Helper

- Task Scheduler

- Telnet

- Themes

- Windows Installer

- Wireless Zero Configuration

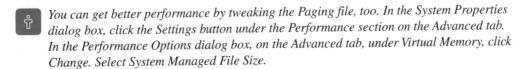 *You can get better performance by tweaking the Paging file, too. In the System Properties dialog box, click the Settings button under the Performance section on the Advanced tab. In the Performance Options dialog box, on the Advanced tab, under Virtual Memory, click Change. Select System Managed File Size.*

6

↘ Use DirectX Diagnostic Tool

Let Microsoft's DirectX Diagnostic Tool see if your computer meets a game's minimum requirements and point out potential problems.

Shopping for games or hardware? Having problems with the installed games or hardware on your system? Let Microsoft's DirectX Diagnostic Tool, located on Microsoft's Windows XP web pages, and possibly already on your computer, help. This diagnostic tool tells you everything you need to know about your system, including information about processor type, installed RAM, the version of DirectX you have, and more. You can then use this information to decide if your computer meets the minimum requirements of the game you want to play, or if additional hardware is required.

In addition to learning about your own system configuration, this tool also lists known and potential problems with your setup, and allows you to test DirectX features, view installed hardware, view network properties, and get DirectX help.

If you aren't sure what DirectX is or does, briefly, its an application programming interface (API) that runs in the background and handles the audio and video content required by your games (and other software). This program helps applications and hardware communicate, and controls low-level functions for hardware, including joysticks, keyboards, mice, and sound and sound output, to name a few.

To use the DirectX Diagnostic Tool:

1. Click Start | Run.

2. In the Run box, type **dxdiag**.

3. Click OK.

The output will look similar to what is shown in Figure 6-8. Here, you can view system resources, test DirectX functionality, diagnose problems, and change configuration options. The DirectX Files tab lists any known problems with your setup. The Display tab offers ways to enhance your gaming experience. Figure 6-8, for instance, shows that the hardware accelerated Direct3D 9+ is not available because the display driver does not support it. That makes sense, because the display adapter and the display are low-end models on this particular computer. Knowing this will allow you to update drivers as necessary to obtain better performance.

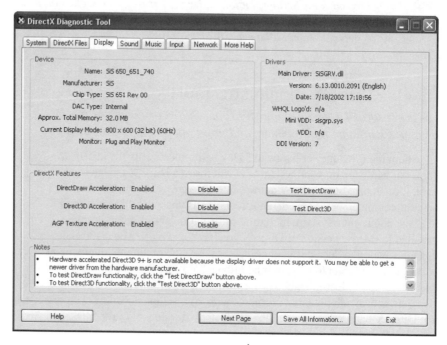

FIGURE 6-8 Use the DirectX Diagnostic Tool to locate problems

If you can't run the DirectX Diagnostic Tool from the Run dialog box, you don't have DirectX 9 installed (and you don't have SP2). DirectX 9 is integrated with Service Pack 2. If you don't want SP2 but you do want DirectX 9, you have to download DirectX 9 independently:

1. Open your web browser and search for Microsoft DirectX 9. Locate the download on the appropriate Microsoft web page. (It may be referred to as DirectX 9.0c End-User Runtime.)

2. Download the application, saving it to your hard drive.

*To see if your computer is ready to play the latest games, visit Microsoft's Windows XP Expert Zone (**http://www.microsoft.com/windowsxp/expertzone/default.mspx**) and search for Windows XP Game Advisor. The application will check your computer's installed hardware and determine if you're ready to play the latest and hottest games on the market.*

HOW SP2 AFFECTS GAMING

By now, you should have SP2 on your computer. (For more on Service Pack 2, see Chapter 5.) That's good, because SP2 offers updates, fixes, and much better security than having no service packs at all, or only SP1. It also offers the newest DirectX features, including DirectX 9, detailed in the previous section. As you know from Chapter 5, it also includes a firewall and additional features. Unfortunately, SP2's firewall can interfere with some games, especially online multiplayer games. To make everything play nice with everything else, you may need to perform a few tweaks to the firewall.

 To benefit from SP2's new DirectX features, you need hardware that supports it.

⟶ Play Safe Online with SP2

SP2's new security features can interfere with online gaming, but you can use the firewall effectively and play games at the same time if you know how.

If you've noticed that you're unable to play online multiplayer games like you used to, or have lost some or all functionality, you need to tweak the Windows Firewall settings or perhaps turn it off completely. Some affected games include Warcraft III and Star Wars: Knights of the Republic. There are many more listed at **http://www.gamespot.com**, and another list is available at Microsoft, in Knowledge Base article 884130. If you have discovered that some of your favorite games don't work as they should, you can either visit those web pages for a workaround or turn off SP2's firewall completely.

Unfortunately, turning off the firewall isn't a good idea if you don't have a backup. If you find yourself in this position, consider downloading a free firewall, like ZoneAlarm, or purchasing a firewall from Symantec or McAfee. Before installing the new program, turn off Windows Firewall and then install and turn on the new one. To turn off Windows Firewall:

1. Disconnect from the Internet.

2. Click Start | Control Panel.

3. Open Windows Firewall.

4. Click Off (Not Recommended), as shown in Figure 6-9, and click OK.

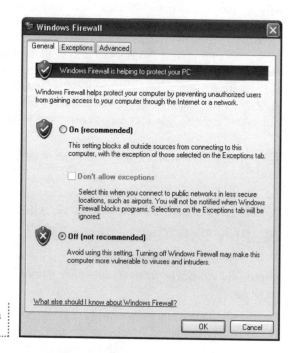

FIGURE 6-9 You can turn off SP2's Windows Firewall if desired.

5. Install and turn on the new firewall.

6. Connect to the Internet for updates from the manufacturer.

If you don't have an additional firewall, you shouldn't turn off Windows Firewall. Instead, you should manually make exceptions if possible, or visit the manufacturer's web site for a documented and safe workaround.

◥ Unblock Games Manually

You can also unblock a game manually, and then play the game without turning off Windows Firewall.

You can add a program to Windows Firewall's Exceptions list manually. You can then play the game without the firewall interfering. Games may have multiple executables, though, so it may take some trial and error to find the correct executable to unblock. You can see all of an application's executables in the program folder.

To unblock a game manually:

1. Click Start | Control Panel, and open Windows Firewall.

2. Click the Exceptions tab. Programs will likely be listed there already, as shown in Figure 6-10. Items that are unchecked have been manually blocked.

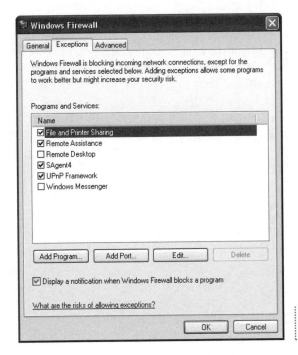

FIGURE 6-10 Some programs may be listed here.

3. To unblock a game, click Add Program.

4. If you can see the program in the Add A Program dialog box, select it and click OK. If the program or its executable file cannot be found, click Browse.

5. If you had to click Browse in Step 4, in the Look In dialog box, choose Local Disk C: (or whatever drive you store your program files on), click Program Files, and locate the program's folder. Select the executable file to unblock, and then click Open.

6. Click OK to add the program.

If you are an advanced user and have set up a game server for a LAN party, you may have to open a range of ports for your players to have access to your computer. In that case, click the Add Port button, and type the required information about the port name and number and whether it is a UDP or TCP port. If all of this sounds like gibberish to you, don't worry about it. You don't need to do it.

That should about do it for getting started with games, and doing a little tweaking for better performance. The next chapter moves forward to graphics and multimedia in general, including backing up music, pictures, and video, using Windows Media Player, and using Movie Maker 2 to create movies with special effects. Time to break out that camera and download some music!

CHAPTER 7
GET THE MOST OUT OF DIGITAL PHOTOS AND MULTIMEDIA

W indows XP, both Home and Professional, comes with many multimedia applications. This chapter looks at three of them: the Picture Tasks options in the My Pictures folder, Windows Media Player, and Windows Movie Maker. Before you start reading, though, make sure you've downloaded and installed the latest service packs, and verify that you have all of the available updates. In particular, make sure you have Windows Media Player 10 and Windows Movie Maker 2 or higher.

 If you need more information about how to use Windows Update to obtain upgrades, revisit Chapter 5.

KEEP PICTURE-PERFECT PICTURES

Digital cameras have become quite popular, and the number of people purchasing and using them is increasing every day. Unfortunately, many people don't fully understand how to organize their pictures or the importance of backing them up regularly. If this sounds like you, you're in luck: these are the first two topics covered in this section.

 If you don't yet have a digital camera, consider purchasing a disposable one from your local retailer. Many retailers even offer free prints and/or picture CDs.

◥ Organize Your Pictures

Don't just leave your pictures scattered all over; organize them in folders and rename them appropriately.

If you just got started in digital photography, organizing your pictures is probably not on your immediate to-do list. On the other hand, if you've been taking and collecting digital pictures for a long time, your My Pictures folder probably looks something like what's shown in Figure 7-1. Either way, without the proper organizational procedures in place, you're going to eventually have a mess on your hands.

There are several ways to organize your images, but the easiest way is to create folders and drag images into them. If your pictures aren't named appropriately, you can rename them before you sort them into folders, too. Once your current pictures are organized, you can continue to use this method as you add images.

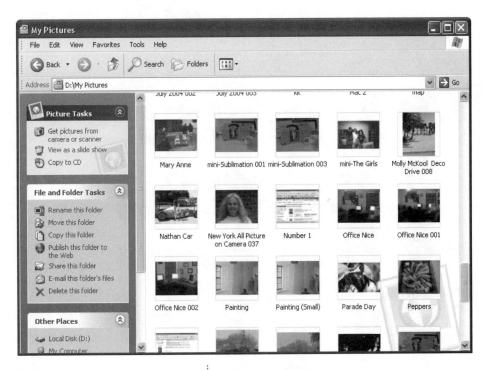

FIGURE 7-1 If you have pictures scattered about, organize them.

To get your pictures organized, you first create folders, then rename your images, and finally drag pictures to the correct folder:

1. Click Start | My Pictures. If My Pictures isn't listed on the Start menu, select My Documents. My Pictures will be inside that folder.

2. Delete any pictures you no longer want. To do this, select the image by hovering the mouse over it, and then click Delete This File from the File And Folder Tasks pane. You can select multiple images by holding down the CTRL key (to select noncontiguous images) or the SHIFT key (to select contiguous images). You can also right-click any picture and choose Delete from the drop-down list.

3. To create a new folder, right-click an empty area inside the My Pictures right pane, point to New, and click Folder. Type a name for the folder and press ENTER. Figure 7-2 shows some sample folders.

4. To rename any image, right-click and choose Rename. Type a new name for the image.

5. To move any image, click and drag it to the appropriate folder. Figure 7-2 shows an organized My Pictures folder.

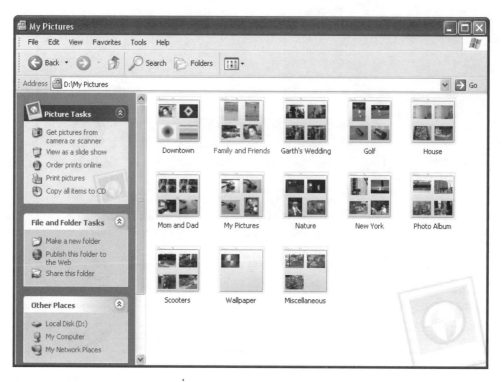

FIGURE 7-2 Name folders descriptively

One other thing to keep in mind when organizing your photos is that, by default, the My Pictures folder is on the C: drive, or whatever drive the operating system was installed on. Many computers these days come with partitioned drives, though, with the OS and applications on the C: drive, and a D: drive for data. If that's the case, you may want to create your own My Pictures folder on the D: drive, and create subfolders inside of that. This is done by using the same method detailed here: right-click anywhere in an empty area of any window, point to New, and click Folder.

Back Up Your Pictures

Backing up your pictures is as important as backing up important documents, diaries, tax information, and music.

If you've taken my advice and placed all of your images in the My Pictures folder and in descriptive subfolders, backing up your data will be a breeze. Backing up is important, too, although most people don't fully understand how important it actually is. Consider this scenario: You store all of your digital pictures on your hard drive, and only print out a few to show friends and family. Some of the others you e-mail or post on the Web. You view the ones you want to see at home as a slideshow. Over the years you collect thousands of pictures. Now, what happens to all of those pictures if the water heater bursts and floods your home? What if your home catches fire or your hard drive crashes? What if you spill a beer on your computer while listening to music? Without a backup, all of the pictures stored on your computer will be lost. You *have* to plan ahead for such disasters.

There are several ways to back up your pictures, just as there are several ways to organize them. If you have a CD burner, though, backing up is simple:

1. Open the My Pictures folder (or any folder or subfolder that contains pictures).

2. Use the mouse to select folders and/or images, as shown in Figure 7-3. You can also choose Edit | Select All to select all of the images in a folder.

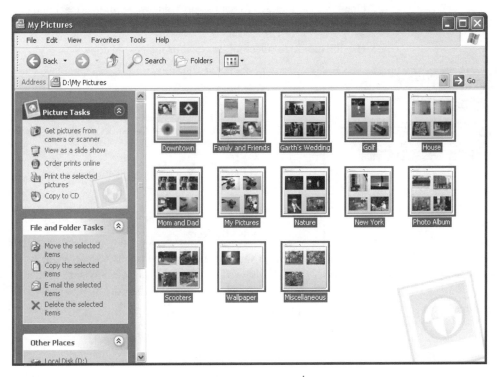

FIGURE 7-3 Select images to copy to a CD

3. Place a blank CD in your CD burner. If prompted about what you'd like to do, select Take No Action.

4. In the Picture Tasks pane, also shown in Figure 7-3, click Copy To CD.

5. Click Start | My Computer, and select the CD-R or CD-RW drive.

6. In the CD Writing Tasks pane, click Write These Files To CD.

7. In the wizard that appears, click Next and Next again to start the process. After the CD Writing Wizard scans the files, continue to work through the wizard, clicking Next each time.

8. Once the CD Writing Wizard completes, the CD will eject and the wizard will close.

If you don't have a CD burner, you can use a similar procedure to copy the items to a secure location for backup. For instance, you can copy the images to another computer on the network, an external hard drive, or a Zip disk:

1. Open the My Pictures folder (or any folder or subfolder that contains pictures).

2. Use the mouse to select folders (and/or images) to copy.

FIGURE 7-4 Use the Copy This Folder command to back up images

3. In the File And Folder Tasks pane, click Copy This Folder.

4. In the Copy Items dialog box, shown in Figure 7-4, select the area to copy the folder or pictures to. Click Copy.

You can also use Windows XP's built-in backup program:

1. Click Start | All Programs | Accessories | System Tools | Backup.

2. If the Advanced Mode opens, select Wizard Mode. If given an option, select Wizard Mode. Click Next to start the wizard.

3. Select Back Up Files And Settings. Click Next.

4. Select Let Me Choose What To Back Up. Click Next.

5. In the Items To Back Up list, shown in Figure 7-5, select the drive that holds the My Pictures folder. Most of the time, this is C: or D:.

6. Locate the My Pictures folder and place a check mark next to it, also shown in Figure 7-5. Click Next.

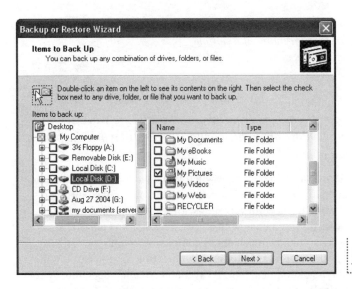

FIGURE 7-5 Locate the My Pictures folder

7. Click Browse to identify where you will save the backup. Unfortunately, the Backup utility can't be used to save a backup to a CD, but you can save it to your desktop, and then create a copy of it on a CD. You may also want to save it to an external hard drive or other backup device.

8. Type a name for the backup, as shown in Figure 7-6. Click Next.

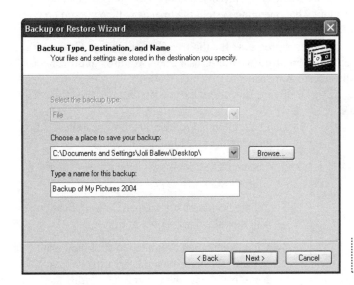

FIGURE 7-6 Choose a place to save and a name for the backup

9. Click Finished, and when the backup is complete, click Close.

You can make backups occur automatically by using the scheduling options in Backup. Check out the Help and Support files for more information.

⬛ Burn Pictures to a CD Anyone Can Watch

Even those friends and family members who still use Windows 98 and don't know diddly about the computer can still enjoy the pictures you've burned on a CD.

There will probably come a time when you have lots of pictures to share, but sending them via e-mail or posting them on the Web just won't do. You might want to share your images with someone who doesn't have an Internet connection, someone with a very slow dial-up connection, or someone who doesn't know much about computers. You might also want to create a slideshow of images for a party, meeting, or convention, not knowing what type of computer will be available, or what operating system. If XP isn't available, it's going to be pretty difficult to get a slideshow of those burned images going.

There's a way around all of these dilemmas: you can burn your images to a CD and add an automatic slideshow program; then, when you or your recipient places the CD in the CD drive, a slideshow of your pictures will begin automatically. There's no need to have an Internet connection, no need to know a ton about computers (specifically, all you need to do is boot up, insert the CD, browse to the correct folder, and open the images), and no need to worry about what operating system the images will be viewed on. This program works with any computer that runs Windows 95 or higher.

So, what's this magic program? It's the free CD Slide Show Generator PowerToy, available from **http://www.microsoft.com/windowsxp/downloads/ powertoys/xppowertoys.mspx**.

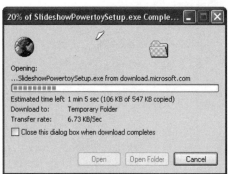

FIGURE 7-7 Download the application first

To use this program, you first have to download it:

1. Open Internet Explorer and browse to the URL listed in the preceding paragraph.

2. Locate CD Slide Show Generator and click Slideshow.exe.

3. When prompted, click Open. The application will download, as shown in Figure 7-7.

4. Click Next when prompted to start the Install Wizard. Work through the wizard, clicking Next, Next, and Next, and finally Finish.

Once the program is installed, just burn a picture CD as directed earlier. Before the CD begins to burn, you'll see one extra wizard page, which prompts you to add a picture viewer. To add the picture viewer so that a slideshow automatically begins when the CD is inserted, and so that the CD can be viewed by anyone with Windows 95 or higher, select Yes, Add A Picture Viewer, as shown in Figure 7-8.

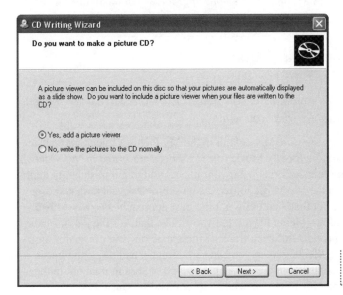

7

FIGURE 7-8 Choose to add a picture viewer when prompted

MY FAVORITE WINDOWS MEDIA PLAYER TIPS

Windows Media Player is included with Windows XP and can be used to play DVDs, music CDs, and homemade movies, and to listen to Internet radio stations. You can also use the player to burn CDs, purchase music, and download music. For the most part, using Windows Media Player is pretty straightforward. You pop in a CD or choose a song from a list, and Windows Media Player does the rest. This section isn't about those things.

This section contains a few of my favorite tips to help you get more from Windows Media Player, such as creating organized playlists and backing up your music. You can never be too organized or too secure. With your music and media organized, you can then concentrate on using that music in new ways.

One of the ways to enhance your music is to apply volume leveling and crossfading to your playlists before you listen to the music or burn your CDs. Volume leveling lets you make sure that the CD doesn't blow you out of the car when a song comes on that was obtained from a different source than your other music. Another way to enhance your music is to apply crossfading, where the songs fade into one another. There are lots of ways to work with Windows Media Player, and in this section, you're going to learn some of my favorites.

 Make sure you've downloaded and installed Windows Media Player 10; version 10 is an upgrade to what ships with Windows XP, and the previous upgrade, Windows Media Player 9.

↘ Arrange Your Music with Automatic Playlists

Once you've acquired music, you'll need to create playlists so you can quickly hear exactly what you want.

Your pictures are stored by default in the My Pictures folder, and music is stored similarly, in the My Music folder. (Videos are stored in My Videos.) Thus, when you think of organizing your music, you might mistakenly think you should open the My Music folder, create subfolders, and drag and drop files into them, but that's actually not the best approach. The My Music folder and Windows Media Player don't work like that; it's the job of Media Player to sift through and keep track of the music on your computer, not yours. Inside the Media Player, you can sort, arrange, and refine the music to your heart's content, but the player has the job of sorting it all out in the background. The only time you need to access the My Music folder is to delete music you no longer want, and even then, there are other ways to do that inside the Media Player. Figure 7-9 shows a sample My Music folder.

Playlists, both the ones created automatically and the ones you create manually, are a vital part of arranging your music using Windows Media Player 10. Once a playlist is created, you can play it at any time and tweak it by adding or deleting tracks at will.

Automatic playlists can be created based on a number of factors, including the following (which is not a complete list):

- Album artist
- Album title
- Artist
- Rating
- Category
- Date added
- Date played

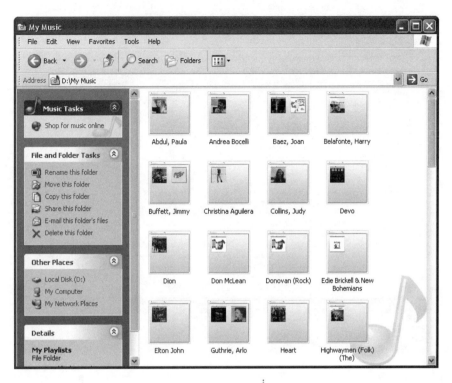

FIGURE 7-9 Music is stored in the My Music folder.

- Mood
- Parental rating
- Publisher
- Title
- Writer

In this section, you'll learn how to create and use automatic playlists; in the following section, you'll create your own. To create an automatic playlist:

1. Open Windows Media Player 10 from Start | All Programs | Accessories | Entertainment | Windows Media Player.

2. Click the Library tab, as shown in Figure 7-10. In this example, All Music is selected, and none of the folders are expanded.

FIGURE 7-10 Open Media Library

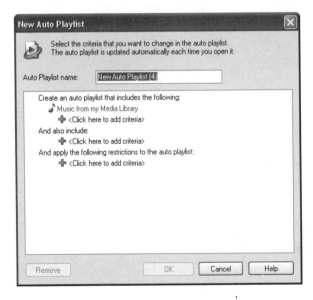

FIGURE 7-11 The New Auto Playlist dialog box offers many options for playlists.

3. Right-click Auto Playlists and choose New. The New Auto Playlist dialog box will open, shown in Figure 7-11.

4. Type a name for the playlist, such as "Songs For July 4th Party" or "Songs For Folk CD." Make sure it is a descriptive name.

5. Under Create An Auto Playlist That Includes The Following, select Click Here To Add Criteria. From the drop-down list that appears under Click Here To Add Criteria, select any criteria. Depending on what you select, you will be prompted to enter more information, again by

clicking the required area. If you choose Album Artist, for instance, you'll be prompted to click to set the artist you want to add. If you select Date Added, you'll be prompted to choose a date, and whether you want to add music acquired before or after it. Repeat this step until all criteria has been added. Figure 7-12 shows the result.

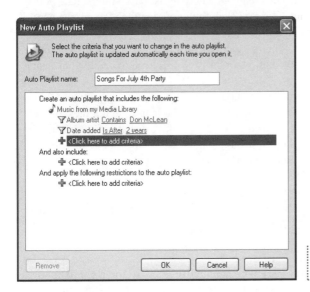

FIGURE 7-12 Add criteria to set auto playlist requirements

6. To add additional criteria, under And Also Include, select Music From My Media Library, and repeat Step 5.

7. To add a restriction regarding number of songs, total duration, or total file size, under And Apply The Following Restrictions To The Auto Playlist, make the appropriate selections. If you're creating a playlist to burn to a CD, make sure the file size of the playlist is limited to under 70MB; if you're creating a playlist for an event that lasts one hour, set the duration.

8. Click OK to create the playlist. The new auto playlist will appear under Auto Playlists in the Media Library.

 Windows Media Player has already created several auto playlists for you, including Have Not Heard Recently, Listen To At Night, and others. The playlist changes each time you start the Media Player, depending on your listening habits.

⬌ Create Your Own Playlists

Get more specific by creating your own playlists manually.

Although auto playlists are a great way to quickly create playlists, they change. For instance, if you create an auto playlist based on the date you added music to the music library, each time you download or copy a new song, that particular playlist will change. Often, this is not an ideal situation. For static playlists that contain specific songs in a specific order, say for a wedding reception, convention, or party, you'll need to create your own playlists.

When you create your own playlists manually, you get to choose the artists and songs. You can also keep track of the length, in minutes, of the playlist, just in case you're trying to create a playlist that meets specific time criteria. As with auto playlists, you name the list, it appears in the Media Library, and you can select it at any time.

To create a playlist:

1. Open Windows Media Player 10 from Start | All Programs | Accessories | Entertainment | Windows Media Player.

2. Click the Library tab.

3. Right-click My Playlists and choose New. In the right pane of Media Player 10, you'll see an empty playlist, as shown in Figure 7-13.

4. Expand All Music, locate the song(s) to add, and select them. Drag the selected song(s) or albums to the New Playlist pane.

5. To name the playlist, click New Playlist and choose Save Playlist As. In the Save As dialog box, shown in Figure 7-14, create a name for the new playlist.

If your Media Library contains songs that require licenses—perhaps you downloaded the songs from Music Now or some other monthly subscription service—Windows Media Player checks for those licenses. If it can't find

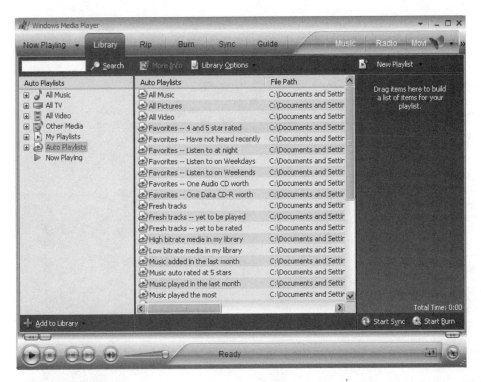

FIGURE 7-13 Create a new playlist

7

FIGURE 7-14 Save the new playlist

the proper licenses, you won't be able to play the song. Figure 7-15 shows a sample playlist with several songs that do not have the required licenses. They are the ones with an exclamation point beside them.

FIGURE 7-15 Exclamation points point out problems with the playlist.

To see error details, right-click the song and choose Error Details. The resulting dialog box offers choices for resolving the problem, whatever it is. If it's due to a lack of licensing, you may want to delete the song from your music library. To delete the song from the library, check Remove File From Library.

Right-clicking a song title also enables you to move the song up or down the list, see the file's properties, and copy the song to a CD or other device.

It Doesn't Always Have to Be Microsoft: Try iTunes!

iTunes, available at **http://www.apple.com/itunes**, lets you purchase music along with the licenses for under a dollar per song. The song will be legally yours; a much better deal than older subscription services. If you prefer to stick with Microsoft, click Music and visit its online store.

7

⬦ Crossfading and Volume Leveling Your Playlists

You can apply effects to your playlists that will enhance your listening experience.

There are a couple of really simple tricks for polishing your playlists, and both are available in Windows Media Player: crossfading and volume leveling. Crossfading simply fades songs into one another, like radio DJs do. The first song fades out as the second one fades in. This is a neat trick when creating CDs or playlists for dances or weddings.

Volume leveling makes sure the songs in your playlists are of equal volume. If you've copied and/or downloaded music from different sources, you'll likely understand the importance of volume leveling. Music recorded from analog sources, Internet radio stations, CDs, and web sites can have varying degrees of *loudness*. When you create and play a playlist or burn a CD with those songs, one song may be too quiet to hear while another may blow you out of your chair!

Incorporating either or both of these technologies can make for interesting CDs and musical experiences. Here's how to enable crossfading:

1. Open Windows Media Player 10 from Start | All Programs | Accessories | Entertainment | Windows Media Player.

2. Right-click the Library tab, point to View | Enhancements, and click Crossfading And Auto Volume Leveling.

3. As shown in Figure 7-16, click Turn On Crossfading (the option changes to Turn Off Crossfading).

4. Move the slider to define how long you want the overlap to last.

5. Click the X in the top-right corner of the Crossfading And Auto Volume Leveling pane to close it.

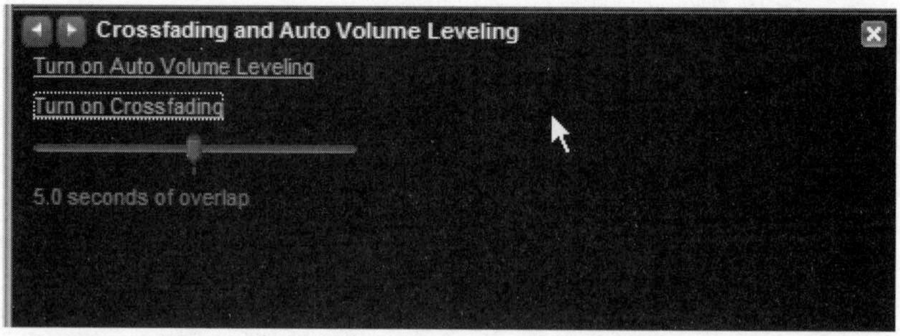

FIGURE 7-16 Turn on crossfading to blend songs together

To enable volume leveling requires a few extra steps. First, the music you want to level out must be stored on your hard drive. As you'd expect, you can't make changes to the volume of songs on a read-only CD from a music store or one that you've burned.

Second, you have to tell Windows Media Player you want to use volume leveling, and let the application assign volume leveling values to your music. Your newest music, the music you added to the Media Library using Windows Media Player, will already have values: they're automatically assigned. But if you have music that is older, or music you acquired while using a different version of the Media Player or a third-party player, you have to tell Windows Media Player 10 to assign values to those files. Since it's difficult to remember where all of your music files came from, this step is recommended at initial setup.

Finally, turn on volume leveling, letting the Media Player know that's what you prefer. From here on out, you'll have volume leveling applied to all of your music.

To add volume leveling and configure your computer to apply it to all music files:

1. Open Windows Media Player 10 from Start | All Programs | Accessories | Entertainment | Windows Media Player.

2. Right-click Library, point to File | Add To Library, and click By Searching Computer.

3. In the Search On list, select All Drives, as shown in Figure 7-17.

4. Click Browse and, in the Browse For Folder dialog box, locate the area of your hard drive where your music files are located. Click OK.

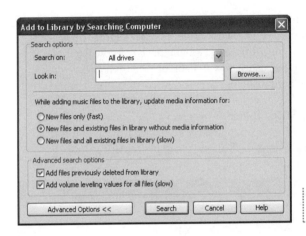

FIGURE 7-17 Choose All Drives for the search option

5. To get the most extensive search and information, click the New Files And All Existing Files In Library (Slow) radio button. Verify that Add Volume Leveling Values For All Files (Slow) is also checked. This is also shown in Figure 7-17. Click Search.

6. Click OK when the Media Player has finished searching for files.

7. Right-click Library, point to View | Enhancements, and click Crossfading And Auto Volume Leveling.

8. In the Enhancements pane, select Turn On Auto Volume Leveling. (If volume leveling is already on, the option says Turn Off Auto Volume Leveling; if that's the case, don't do anything.)

◥ Back Up Your Music

Just like backing up photos and other data, backing up your music and their licenses is important.

If your computer crashes and you don't have a backup of the My Music folder, you lose everything you previously copied or downloaded. You lose all of your licenses too. Chances are you have some sort of backup now, though, perhaps some songs copied to your iPod or other portable music player, and maybe some CDs you've burned to listen to in your car. However, you might not have a full backup or a backup of your licenses. It's best to take the time to do that now, just in case.

As with backing up pictures, you can burn your music files to a CD or Zip disk by dragging and dropping (just keep track of the size of the files), copy them to an external hard drive, or use the Windows Backup utility to copy to your own hard drive, a network drive, or other source. However, backing up licenses is a little different, and you have to know the trick.

Take a look first at the easiest way to back up your music, by copying the data to an external hard disk:

1. Open the My Music folder. It may be on the C: drive in the My Documents folder, or it may be on another partition in a folder you've created. Figure 7-18 shows a sample folder.

FIGURE 7-18 A sampling of music

2. Click Edit | Select All.

3. In the File And Folder Tasks pane, choose Copy The Selected Items.

4. In the Copy Items dialog box, browse to the location in which to copy the files. Click Copy.

There are other options, of course, and they are detailed earlier in this chapter in the "Keep Picture-Perfect Pictures" section. From inside the

My Music folder, in the Music Tasks pane, you can
select Copy To Audio CD, for instance, and you can
select multiple files to copy multiple items. You can
also use the Windows Backup utility. If you choose
to back up to a CD, though, be extra vigilant. Music
files can be quite large. To see just how large, hover
the mouse over any folder or song in the My Music
folder. The information about the size will appear.
Remember, CDs generally only hold 70MB, so when
you are selecting songs to burn, make sure to stay
under that limit. You can also see a file or folder's
size by right-clicking and choosing Properties.
The Arlo Guthrie Properties dialog box is shown in
Figure 7-19. Notice this single folder is 31.9MB.

Once your music is backed up, you'll want to
back up your licenses. Licenses are what allow you
to play music you've purchased and downloaded.
To back up your licenses, which will often fit on
a floppy disk:

FIGURE 7-19 The Properties
dialog box is one way to find
a folder's size.

1. Open Windows Media Player 10 from Start | All
   Programs | Accessories | Entertainment | Windows
   Media Player.

2. Right-click Library, point to Tools, and
   click Manage Licenses. The Manage
   Licenses dialog box opens, as shown in
   Figure 7-20.

3. Click Change to browse to the area in
   which to save the backup. This can be
   a network drive, your own hard drive,
   or even a floppy drive. (If you save to
   your own hard drive, though, remember
   to burn that to a CD or other removable
   media.) Click OK when done.

4. Click Back Up Now. Click OK when finished.

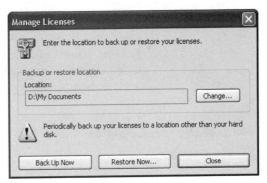

FIGURE 7-20 Back up licenses regularly

*If your system has the capability, backing up using DVDs is a better option than CDs
because DVDs hold much more data.*

MOVIES AND MOVIE MAKER 2

With your pictures and music in order, you are ready to take a look at movies. Movie Maker 2 is the application you'll use to create movies from footage you take with your digital video (DV) camera. Movie Maker 2 walks you through the process for the most part, offering options in the Movie Tasks pane to lead you, and offering wizards where applicable. In the Movie Tasks pane, you can perform the following tasks, among others:

- Capture footage from your DV camera
- Import video, pictures, audio, and music
- View and add video effects and transitions
- Make an AutoMovie
- Save movies to your computer or to a CD
- Send a movie in an e-mail

I'll assume you have your camera connected and working, that you've taken some footage, and that you know how to use Movie Maker 2 to import that footage. If you need more information about or assistance with those tasks, there are plenty of Help and Support files available from the Help menu.

What I want to cover here are some tips and tricks for getting a movie made quickly, while still offering a professional-looking output. This includes using AutoMovie, personalizing your movie-in-progress with transitions and effects, adding title pages and credits, and exploring different ways to share your movies with others.

 Make sure you've downloaded and installed Windows Movie Maker 2; version 2 is an upgrade to what ships with Windows XP.

⇘ Use AutoMovie to Make a Movie on the Go

Make a movie on the run with AutoMovie.

There are lots of reasons you'd need to create a movie quickly. Perhaps you forgot about an assignment at work or school, need to give immediate feedback on a game or production you are in charge of or have filmed, or need to distribute footage from some kind of outing to all members right away. You may want to get footage of your newborn to all of your relatives before the baby starts walking. Whatever the case, with AutoMovie, you can create a movie quickly.

As with any movie in Movie Maker 2, you need to connect the DV camera and import the footage. Figure 7-21 shows an example of how your interface should look. Notice that the Movie Tasks pane is selected; if yours isn't showing, click the Tasks button on the Standard toolbar.

FIGURE 7-21 Setting up Movie Maker 2 for an AutoMovie

Once you have your video footage ready, it's time to make an AutoMovie:

1. Open Movie Maker from Start | All Programs | Accessories | Entertainment | Windows Movie Maker.

2. In the Movie Tasks pane, shown in Figure 7-21, under Edit Movie, click Make An AutoMovie.

3. Select from the five AutoMovie styles: Flip and Slide, Highlights Movie, Music Video, Old Movie, or Sports Highlights. Beside each is a description. In this example, we'll create a clean, simple movie, with cuts, fades, a title, and credits. Therefore, select Highlights Movie.

4. In the Select An AutoMovie Editing Style dialog box, shown in Figure 7-22, scroll down and locate More Options. Here, you'll enter a title and select background music. Click Enter A Title For The Movie.

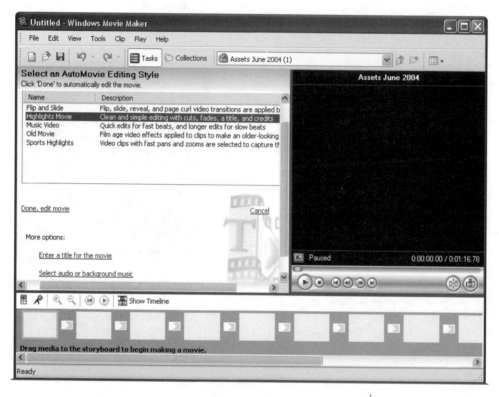

FIGURE 7-22 Locate More Options to add a title and select background music

5. In the Enter Text For Title area, type the text to add.

6. Under More Options, choose Select Audio Or Background Music.

7. In the Add Audio Or Background Music area, either browse to the location of the music file or choose None for no music. For now, leave the Audio Levels at their default settings.

8. Click the Done, Edit Movie option. Movie Maker 2 analyzes the video footage and creates the movie automatically.

9. When AutoMovie is finished, click File | Save Project As, name the project, and click Save. I prefer to save the projects in a subfolder of My Videos called Project Files.

If you wanted to, you could select Save Movie File from the File menu instead of Save Project As. The difference between the two is not subtle. A project can be further edited; a movie cannot. The movie is the final product; the project is a work in progress. Because we'll be doing more editing in the next section, it's best to leave this project saved as a project. In the last section, you'll learn several ways to save the final product in the form of a movie.

⮧ Personalize Your Movie

No matter how you got your project to where it is, manually or using AutoMovie, you can personalize it with transitions, effects, still pictures, and text pages.

You can personalize your movie in a number of ways, including adding video transitions between clips, incorporating video effects into clips, and adding still pictures and/or pages that contain text between clips. That's just the tip of the iceberg, though. As you progress with Movie Maker 2, you'll learn to do much more. You'll see some of these other options as you work through this section; feel free to experiment with those options along the way.

In the following tutorial, you'll learn the easiest and fastest ways to import still pictures, import music, and add video effects, video transitions, and title and credit pages. All of these will add depth to your movie and make it more enjoyable. The best part, though, is that you'll learn the shortcuts for doing it quickly.

1. Open Movie Maker from Start | All Programs | Accessories | Entertainment | Windows Movie Maker.

2. Click File | Open Project. Locate the project saved in the previous example (or any project in progress) and click Open. The clips created by Movie Maker will automatically be added to the storyboard or timeline. Figure 7-23 shows an example using the storyboard. (This particular footage is for a *Home Documentation Video of Assets* movie for my own protection and my insurance company.)

3. To add a still picture, in the Movie Tasks pane, select Import Pictures. In the Import File window, browse to My Pictures, and double-click any picture. The picture will appear in the Collections pane; simply drag it to the storyboard to add it. Figure 7-24 shows a new image added to the end of the project in this example.

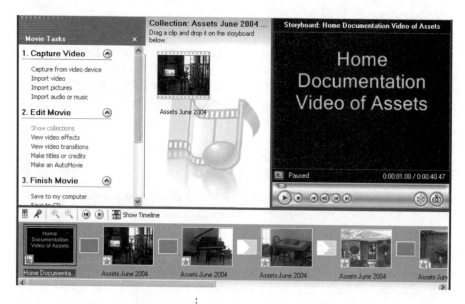

FIGURE 7-23 Movie Maker 2's basic project layout

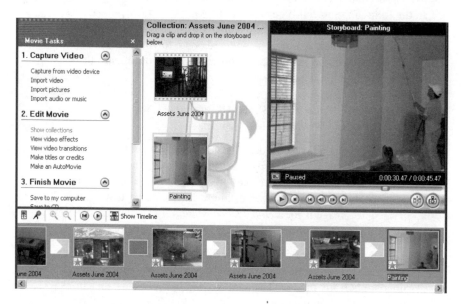

FIGURE 7-24 Add still pictures quickly by dragging and dropping

4. To add background music, in the Movie Tasks pane, select Import Audio Or Music. In the Import File window, browse to My Music, and double-click any song. The music will appear in the Collections pane; simply drag it to the storyboard to add it. Since audio clips can only be added in timeline view, the interface will switch if necessary. Figure 7-25 shows a music track added to the project in this example and the new timeline view.

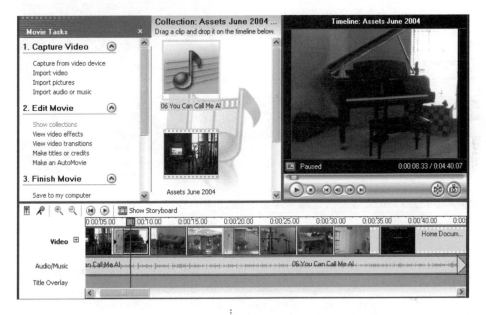

FIGURE 7-25 Add music quickly by dragging and dropping

5. To add video effects, click Show Storyboard. The Show Storyboard button is shown in Figure 7-25, in the bottom pane. It's easier to drag and drop using this interface. Next, under Edit Movie in the Movie Tasks pane, select View Video Effects. Choose any effect and drag and drop the effect onto any clip. Brightness, Increase and Brightness, Decrease are good options for many clips, as are Ease In and Ease out. Once video effects are added, a star will appear in the clip, as shown in Figure 7-26.

6. To add video transitions, verify that storyboard is selected, as in Step 5. Next, under Edit Movie in the Movie Tasks pane, select View Video Transitions. Choose any transition and drag and drop it in between any two clips. Transitions are applied when the clips change. Transitions are denoted in the boxes between clips, as shown in Figure 7-26. Click the Play button to view the effects so far.

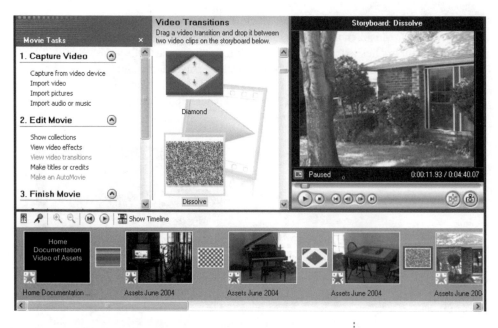

FIGURE 7-26 Add effects and transitions quickly by dragging and dropping

7. To add another text, title, or credit page, under Edit Movie, select Make Titles Or Credits. Under Where Do You Want To Add A Title?, make the appropriate choice. You can add a title page (to add text before, on, or after any clip, select the clip before making a choice):

■ At the beginning of the movie

■ Before the selected clip

■ To the selected clip

■ After the selected clip

■ At the end of the movie

When finished, click Done, Edit Movie.

With your project complete, you can now create the movie and share it with others.

◥ Share Your Movie with Others

Sharing the movie is the best part of making it, and there are lots of ways available.

There are five ways to share your movie using Movie Maker 2. You can save the movie to your computer, save it to a recordable CD, or save as a specific file format (for e-mail, the Web, or for playback on your DV camera). Each has pros and cons, of course. You wouldn't want to send an hour-long movie to a friend via e-mail, for instance, since burning to a CD would be a better choice, just as you wouldn't want to save and distribute a two-minute video of your garage band on a CD when placing it on a web site would be more efficient.

Because choosing how and where to save can sometimes be a little tricky, here are a few thoughts on the saving options for particular movie types (you'll see these options in the upcoming Figure 7-27 too):

- **My Computer**   Save the movie to your computer when you want to burn it to a CD later, view the movie only on the computer, or share the movie and view it later on any networked computer.

- **Recordable CD**   Save the movie to a recordable CD when you want to mail it to a friend, take it with you to a gathering, give it to someone, or archive it.

- **E-Mail**   Save the movie in this format when you plan to e-mail it. Movies sent via e-mail must be extremely short, generally no more than a minute or two in length.

- **The Web**   Save the movie for the Web when you have a short movie and plan to put in on the Internet or save it to a Pocket PC or smartphone. These movies must be short, generally only a few minutes.

- **DV Camera**   Save the movie in this format when you plan to record the finished movie back to the DV camera and a DV camera tape. Tapes make so-so archive options but offer a good way to take a movie with you when there are no other alternatives. For instance, with a DV camera, you can view the movie at a backyard party, where no computer is available.

Once you've decided how you want to save and share the movie, making the movie is a snap:

1. Click File | Save Movie File to open the Save Movie Wizard dialog box, shown in Figure 7-27. Make the appropriate choice and click Next.

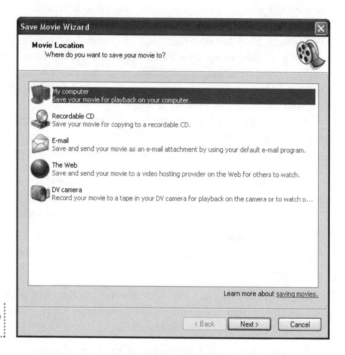

FIGURE 7-27 Choose how to save the movie

2. Enter a filename for the movie and, if necessary, browse to the location in which to save the movie. If necessary, place a blank CD in the CD-R drive or connect the DV camera to the computer. Click Next.

3. Depending on your choice in Step 1, you'll be prompted on how to proceed. If you chose e-mail, there won't be much else to do. If you chose My Computer, you'll need to select quality options. For the most part, the defaults and the recommended options are best. However, in specific circumstances, configuring advanced options is required. Configuring other options is achieved by selecting Other Settings in the Movie Settings dialog box, as shown in Figure 7-28. There, you can select the exact type of movie you need. In this figure, Video For Pocket PC 2003 is selected.

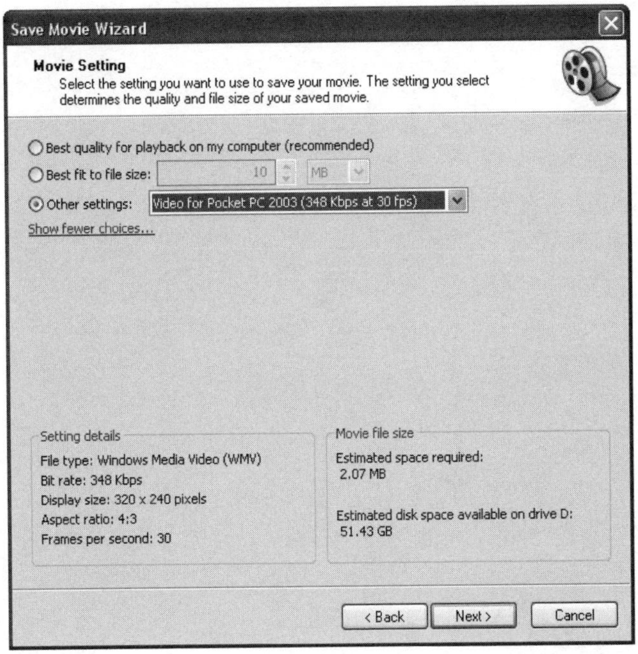

FIGURE 7-28 Generally, the defaults and recommended options are fine, but other options are available.

4. Click Next and wait for the movie to be rendered.

That about covers it for getting your media organized quickly and efficiently. Getting your pictures in folders, your music organized in playlists, and your movies created and saved, and then backing up all of those items is quite a task! With that done, you can now concentrate on other things.

Next, you'll learn about networking. If you have another computer in the house, such as a Media Center, sharing files among those computers can greatly enhance how often you can enjoy them. In the upcoming chapter, you'll learn about wireless networking, troubleshooting the network with command-line tools, and firewalls. Stay tuned!

CHAPTER 8
NETWORKING: GETTING (AND STAYING) CONNECTED

Whether you already have a network in place or not, you're going to benefit from this chapter. Here, you'll learn the least complicated and quickest way to physically set up a home network, how to share a single Internet connection among everyone on the network, and how to use the Network Setup Wizard. The Network Setup Wizard can be used to repair a network, too, in addition to configuring it. Some people simply connect their computers to a hub and wait for them to magically "see" each other, but never formally engineer their network. When a network is set up this way, problems usually occur. These problems can be solved by running the wizard.

With a network set up, you'll learn the most efficient way to share data, media, and hardware, among all users and computers. Sharing media is great for those who have a media center set up in a family room, and for avoiding storing the same items (like vacation pictures) on multiple computers in the home. Storing duplicate items on a network wastes valuable hard drive space.

You'll also learn how to enhance security of shared folders, and the options available for both Windows XP Home and Professional. Finally, you'll learn some command-line tricks for troubleshooting the network when something goes wrong.

GET CONNECTED: THE HOME NETWORK

If you have two or more computers, you can create a network for sharing resources and data. There are several ways to create a network:

- **Connect the computers using a networking device (hub, switch, or router), network interface cards, and cables**   This is a good way to create a very effective and secure small or home business workgroup.

- **Configure a network using Windows Server 2003**   This is an OS that's used to create larger networks called *domains*. Domains, though more secure, are much more difficult to configure and maintain than workgroups, and setting them up is generally the job of a network administrator or certified technician. In addition, they are mostly used in larger companies and corporations who have the resources and know-how to maintain such.

- **Create a wireless network**   This requires purchasing the hardware separately, and then installing and configuring it. At this time, most computers ship with the wired network in mind.

For the simplest, most efficient, and easy-to-manage network possible, most current home and small business users choose the first option, the wired workgroup. The hardware is inexpensive, the setup is simple, and the software for setting up the network is included with Windows XP. Moving from this workgroup to wireless later is an option, but almost all computers these days come with the required hardware for the wired option.

⬎ Get Physical with Wired Networks

There are lots of ways to network computers; choose the easiest and most efficient option.

If you're looking for the fastest, easiest, and least expensive way to put together a network, look no further. If you have a network that's set up with a network server and it's giving you fits, consider switching. In this section, you'll learn all you need to know to put a workgroup together quickly. With the proper hardware, you'll be up and running in no time.

You'll need to verify that each computer you want to connect has a network card. To find out:

1. Either from the Start menu or from the Desktop, right-click My Computer and choose Properties.

2. In System Properties, click the Hardware tab.

3. Under the Device Manager section, select Device Manager.

4. In the Device Manager window, click the View menu, and verify that Devices By Type is selected. If it isn't, select it.

5. Locate Network Adapters and expand it, as shown in Figure 8-1.

6. Look for something that is called a NIC (network interface card). If you can't find this, you don't have a NIC installed.

7. If you locate the NIC but it has a red X or a yellow exclamation point beside it, right-click the item and click Install. If that doesn't work, right-click the item and click Update Driver. If the card still doesn't show up properly in Device Manager, use Windows Update or visit your manufacturer's web site for upgraded drivers or software. If the card still won't work, it may be nonfunctional, and you may need to replace it.

If you have a computer you want to connect that does not have a NIC or has a nonfunctioning NIC, you'll have to install a new one. If you've installed a card before, you can probably install this one. If you've never opened the

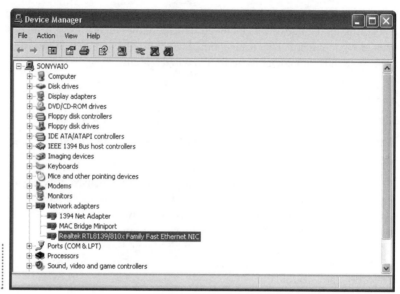

FIGURE 8-1 Determine if a network interface card is installed

computer, you're better off taking it to a technician. For most newer Windows XP computers, you'll be looking for a 10/100 Ethernet NIC for a PCI slot. However, if you aren't sure, take it to a service technician or computer store.

Once all of your computers have NICs, you need to purchase a networking device (hub, switch, or router) and some Ethernet cables. The hub, switch, or router is a small piece of hardware that plugs into a wall outlet. It has inputs for connecting the Ethernet cables. The cables run from the networking device to the computer's NIC. Thus, you'll need one networking device, a NIC, and an Ethernet cable for each computer you plan to connect.

 Visit your local computer store and speak with a salesperson for more information on the available hardware.

Finally, your Internet service provider (ISP) may set up your network for free. If you have broadband or DSL, the company may provide a router and send a technician to your house to set it up. In most instances, they'll also set up a wireless connection between that router and the other computers in your home, *if* you have the required hardware. If that's the case, you need not worry about it yourself.

⬊ Share and Share Alike: Internet Connection Sharing

There's no need to have multiple Internet accounts or connections for every computer on the network; just turn on Internet Connection Sharing.

Once your computers are networked, you can share a single computer's Internet connection with all members on that network. In the old days, you had to have an Internet connection and account for each computer in the home, but not anymore. If you're still running a setup like that, it's time to move forward. If you've just networked a second computer, it's time to get that one connected to the Internet.

The first decision you'll make is what computer is going to be the host. The host should meet the following requirements:

- It should be running Windows XP Home or Professional.

- It must be set up to run most of the time. If the computer is not on, others on the network will not have Internet access.

- If more than one computer meets the first two requirements, but also has DSL, broadband, or a cable modem, choose the fastest computer as the host.

Each network computer that will share this connection must meet the following requirements:

- It must have a NIC and be able to connect to the network.

- If it has Internet Sharing capabilities, they must be disabled.

- It must be running Windows 98 or higher.

To enable Internet Connection Sharing on the designated host computer (or to disable it on any other computer on the network that is not acting as the host):

1. Open Network Connections. There are two ways: right-click My Network Places and choose Properties; or from Control Panel, select Network And Internet Connections (if in Category Mode), and then choose Network Connections.

2. Decide which connection is the connection to the Internet. It won't be the Local Area Connection. Figure 8-2 shows a variety of choices. The correct choice in this instance is under Dial-Up and is named, appropriately, Internet.

FIGURE 8-2 Select the connection to the Internet

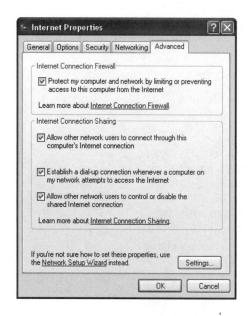

3. Right-click this connection and choose Properties.

4. In the Internet Properties dialog box, click the Advanced tab, as shown in Figure 8-3.

5. Under Internet Connection Sharing, check Allow Other Network Users To Connect Through This Computer's Internet Connection. Depending on your preferences, enable or do not enable the other two choices. Each has to do with how much control over this connection other network users will have.

6. When finished, click OK.

FIGURE 8-3 Enable Internet Connection Sharing

↘ Use the Network Setup Wizard

If you're setting up the network for the first time or just need to repair the network you have, use the Network Setup Wizard.

After your network is set up physically, you can use the Network Setup Wizard to configure it virtually. There are alternate ways to set up the network, but this is by far the fastest and easiest. For the best network performance possible, you should follow the setup directions to the letter.

If you already have a network set up but are having problems with it, running the wizard again may also solve these problems. The Network Setup Wizard locates your shared Internet connection, enables the Internet Connection Firewall, enables and configures a network bridge if the Windows XP computer has more than one NIC, and gives you the opportunity to name (or resolve naming problems for) each computer on the network. (A network will fail if more than one computer has the same name.) Once the network is set up (or connected), you can then share files and folders, share media, play games on the network, and surf the Web simultaneously on all computers in the house.

 The Network Setup Wizard can be run on computers installed with Windows 98, Windows 98SE, Windows Me, and Windows XP Home or Professional. It cannot be run on Windows 2000 or Windows 2003 Server editions. There is information in the help files to add the latter.

Before starting the Network Setup Wizard, verify that you've chosen a computer to act as the host and supply the shared Internet connection. The host should be the one connected to the Internet and thus should be a single computer, as detailed in the previous section. Then, do the following:

- ■ Verify that all hardware is installed on each computer and that it is working properly.

- ■ Turn on all computers, printers, scanners, etc.

- ■ At the host computer, connect to the Internet.

With that done, work your way through the wizard. At the host computer:

1. Choose Start | All Programs | Accessories | Communications | Network Setup Wizard. Click Next to begin.

2. Read the Before You Continue page, and click Next.

3. Since you're configuring the host computer, on the Select A Connection Method page, select This Computer Connects Directly To The Internet. The Other Computers On My Network Connect To The Internet Through This Computer. Click Next.

4. On the Select Your Internet Connection page, choose the connection that you use to access the Internet. It may be chosen already, as shown in Figure 8-4. In this figure, there are three: an Internet connection that uses a modem, a 1394 FireWire connection for a digital video (DV) camera, and a local area connection using a NIC. Click Next.

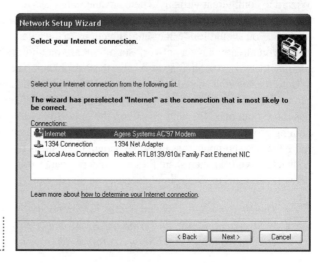

FIGURE 8-4 Select the shared connection for the Internet

5. If your host computer has multiple connections, you can either let the wizard decide what's best for you, or configure the settings yourself. It's wisest to choose Let Me Choose The Connections To My Network. If you're wary of doing it yourself, though, choose Determine The Appropriate Connections For Me (Recommended) and skip to Step 7.

6. On the Select The Connections To Bridge page, select the local area connection that connects your host computer to the others on your network. Uncheck the others. In Figure 8-5, the FireWire connection is unchecked because it is not the connection for the LAN; the NIC is. Click Next.

7. On the next wizard page, type a computer description if desired, and a computer name. The computer's name must be distinct on the network. Click Next.

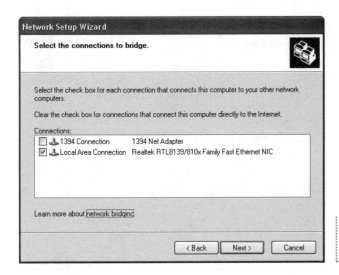

FIGURE 8-5 Select only the connection(s) that are used to connect to the LAN

8. On the Name Your Network page, select a workgroup name. By default, that name is MSHOME. If you're repairing a network and don't know the current workgroup name, click Start, right-click My Computer, choose Properties, and then click the Computer Name tab. The workgroup name will be there. Click Next.

9. Click Next to begin the process of applying your network settings.

Once that's complete, the next step is to get the appropriate network setup files on the other computers in your network. In my opinion, the easiest and most reliable choice is to create a floppy disk and carry it from computer to computer. You can also use the Windows XP CD, but sometimes that's not available, especially with computers purchased from retail computer chains, where computers come with "restore disks" instead of the actual Windows XP CD. So, when prompted with the screen shown in Figure 8-6, select Create A Network Setup Disk. (If your newer computers don't have floppy drives, you'll have to use the Windows XP CD, or choose Create A Network Setup Disk, save the files to your hard drive, burn them onto a CD-R, and use that for the setup disk.)

Depending on the choice you make on the page shown in Figure 8-6, the wizard continues in one of various directions. If you've chosen to create a floppy disk, you'll need to choose the drive, format the disk, and make the copy. If you've chosen to use the Windows XP CD, there isn't much left to do but prepare the other computers.

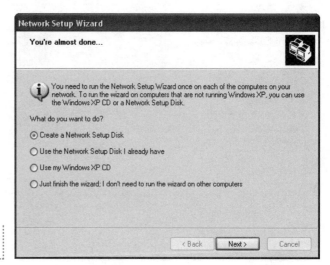

FIGURE 8-6 Decide how to set up the other computers on the network

For the other computers on the network:

1. Insert the network setup disk into the floppy drive.

2. Click Start | My Computer, and select the disk.

3. Double-click netsetup.

4. If you're using a CD, input the CD, select Perform Additional Tasks and then Set Up A Home Or Small Office Network.

5. You'll work your way through the wizard the exact same way as before, except in the dialog box that asks you to define your connection, shown in Figure 8-7, choose This Computer Connects To The Internet Through Another Computer On My Network Or Through A Residential Gateway.

After all computers have been configured, at each computer, open My Network Places. In the Network Tasks pane, select View Workgroup Computers. Each computer should appear within 15 minutes. If a specific computer does not appear, verify that the connections are secure, and run the Network Setup Wizard again on it. Figure 8-8 shows a successful and functional network setup.

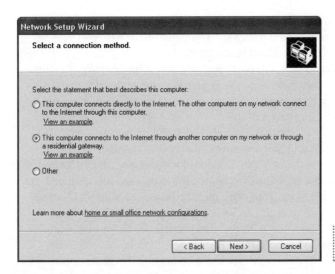

FIGURE 8-7 Setting up the other computers requires different choices.

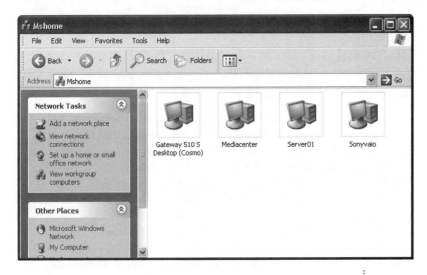

FIGURE 8-8 Network complete

SHARE FILES, FOLDERS, MEDIA, AND HARDWARE

Once your network is set up and working properly, you can begin sharing data and hardware. There are multiple reasons for sharing: to get rid of floppy, Zip, and CD-R disks for transferring data among computers; to save hard disk space by avoiding duplicate files; and to eliminate the need for multiple printers and other hardware. From any computer on the network, you can access any shared data or shared hardware easily.

Once folders and their data are shared, you can set permissions for them. You can change what users who access your data are allowed to do. If you have Windows XP Professional, you can also set simple share permissions to state whether users can have full control over your shared data, change your data, or only read your data. You can also apply NTFS permissions. NTFS permissions allow you to have more control over your own data, regarding who accesses what and how. Control options for documents, media, and other data include permissions to modify and/or write to the data you've shared, list folder contents, and more. Your drive must be formatted with NTFS to do this. As for hardware, you can decide who can have what kind of control when using it. For instance, with a shared printer, you can decide who can manage the printer, who can manage documents, and who can only print. This enables you to avoid having others delete documents in the queue or perform other printing maintenance tasks.

⬊ Avoid a Common Problem: Duplicate Files

Share files, folders, and media so they can be viewed and edited from any computer on the network.

One of the main problems with multiple-computer households is duplicate data. Junior creates a movie of his garage band and tweaks it on his computer in Movie Maker 2, then saves it. He then sends the data to a shared folder for all of his family members to see, but does not delete it from its original location. This happens with family photos too, especially vacation pictures. Everyone has a digital camera, has pictures stored on their own hard drive, and has spread multiple copies all around. This problem is also common with attachments received via e-mail. Instead of saving the funny picture of the dog in the dress to the hard drive in a shared location, the picture is forwarded via e-mail to everyone. It's then on everyone's hard drive instead of in a single, shared location.

Because of the massive amount of duplicate data on most home networks, it's best to take control right away, creating shared folders on each computer or learning how to access the default ones, and put all data to be shared in it.

The first step is to create a folder on the host computer that you will use to share data with everyone on the network:

1. Right-click an empty area of the Desktop, point to New, and click Folder. Name the folder.

2. Right-click the folder and choose Sharing And Security. You'll see the folder's Properties dialog box.

3. The Properties dialog box shown in Figure 8-9 is the one you'll see if you have Windows XP Professional and have Simple File Sharing disabled. If that's the case, check Share This Folder On The Network, and click OK. If you see what's shown in Figure 8-10, you're either using Windows XP Home Edition or using Windows XP Professional with Simple File Sharing enabled. If that's the case, select Share This Folder. (You'll learn more about Simple File Sharing in the next two sections.)

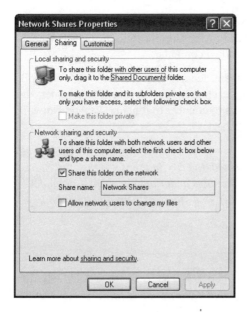

8

FIGURE 8-9 Creating a share using Simple File Sharing

FIGURE 8-10 Creating a share without Simple File Sharing

4. Move what you want to share into this folder.

At each of the networked computers, create a link to this folder (all files stored here by you on your computer can be accessed by anyone on the network):

1. Click Start | Control Panel and, if in Category view, select Network And Internet Connections. Select My Network Places. If in Classic view, select My Network Places in the Other Places pane.

2. In the Network Tasks pane, select Add A Network Place. Click Next to start the wizard.

FIGURE 8-11 Browse for the shared file

3. When prompted, select Choose Another Network Location, and click Next.

4. In the Add Network Place Wizard, click Browse.

5. In the Browse For Folder dialog box, shown in Figure 8-11, expand Entire Network | Microsoft Windows Network. Locate your workgroup name and expand that, and then select the computer that holds the shared folder. Click OK.

6. Click Next, type a name for the new network place, and click Finish. The file can now be accessed on the networked computer.

7. Repeat these steps for each computer on the network, allowing each user to create one shared folder, and the others to connect to it using the Add Network Place Wizard.

 Windows XP comes with shared folders already created, too. To find those, right-click Start, choose Explore All Users, expand Documents And Settings under the Local Disk, expand All Users, and select Shared Documents. Share this folder, and others only need to link to this folder to have access to items you put there.

⇘ Simple Security with Simple File Sharing

You can apply security effortlessly to your shared folders with Simple File Sharing.

As mentioned briefly in the previous section, there are two technologies for applying permissions to shared folders. If you have Windows XP Home Edition, you only have one choice: use Simple File Sharing. If you have Windows XP Professional and your hard drive is formatted with NTFS, you have a second choice: disable Simple File Sharing, configure your own share permissions, and use NTFS advanced permissions. Looking back at Figures 8-9 and 8-10, you can see the difference in the options.

Simple File Sharing is a security setting that's either on or off. If it's on, the folder is shared and you have a few basic choices for how you'll share it. If it's off, there's no sharing of the folder. When you turn off Simple File Sharing, you have access to more options. Specifically, you can state which users or groups of users can do what to the folder and its contents. While this offers a higher level of security and options, it's easy to mess up. It's up to you to decide what you'd rather use. I suggest starting with Simple File Sharing enabled, and if you decide later you need more options, disable it and use the advanced security features.

To apply security using Simple File Sharing, you first need to verify that Simple File Sharing is enabled. Of course, this only applies to users of Windows XP Professional, since it is enabled by default on Windows XP Home Edition and is the only choice:

1. Open Control Panel and, if in Category view, select Appearance And Themes. Select Folder Options.

2. On the View tab, shown in Figure 8-12, make sure Use Simple File Sharing (Recommended) is checked. Click OK.

To apply Simple File Sharing permissions:

1. Locate the folder to share from the Desktop or by using Windows Explorer. To locate a folder in Windows Explorer, right-click Start, choose Explore All Users, expand Documents And Settings, look under your username, and locate the folder to share.

2. Right-click the folder and click Sharing And Security.

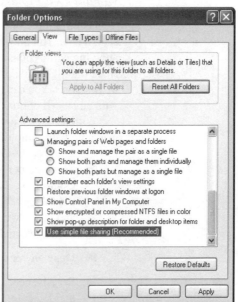

FIGURE 8-12 Enable Simple File Sharing

3. On the Sharing tab, check Share This Folder On The Network. To give permission for other users on the network to change the files in the folder, also check Allow Network Users To Change My Files.

4. You can also choose to drag the folder selected to the Shared Documents folder. To do that, click Shared Documents, wait for the Shared Documents window to open, and drag the folder into it. After doing so, anyone who logs onto your computer using any user account can access the data as well.

5. If you did not perform Step 4, click OK to apply the changes in the Properties dialog box.

⬎ Working Without a Net: Disabling Simple File Sharing

If Simple File Sharing doesn't offer enough security, you can turn it off and set sharing and security permissions yourself, if you're using Windows XP Professional and NTFS.

Using Simple File Sharing isn't the only way to apply security to your shared data. You may have noticed that there aren't too many options for applying permissions with that setup. With Simple File Sharing, you either share the file or you don't. You either let people make changes to your data or you don't. You can create more meaningful permissions configurations with advanced options.

With advanced options, you can do the following, none of which are available with Simple File Sharing:

- Set share permissions to define exactly what users can do: Full Control lets users change set permissions and take ownership of the folder; Change lets users add files and subfolders, change data, and delete data; and Read allows the user to read the data, view filenames, and run program files inside the folder.

- Deny any permission listed in the preceding bullet.

- Set advanced permissions (allow or deny), including Modify, Read and Execute, List Folder Contents, and Write, among others.

- Define what groups and/or users have access to the folder, and what permissions they have.

Unfortunately, there's a right way and a wrong way to apply these advanced permissions, and even the savviest of network technicians have been known to mess it up. Technicians take week-long and month-long training classes just to learn how. Usually, the process consists of creating groups, adding users to those groups, and then applying permission using the groups created. Unfortunately, once advanced permissions are muddled, it's pretty difficult to straighten them out. Since I don't have room here to give you a crash course on all of that, it's best to tread carefully, and take small steps when configuring and applying advanced permissions.

The first step to applying advanced permissions is to disable Simple File Sharing in Windows XP Professional:

1. Open Control Panel and, if in Category view, select Appearance And Themes. Select Folder Options.

2. On the View tab, make sure Use Simple File Sharing (Recommended) is unchecked. Click OK.

To apply advanced permissions after Simple File Sharing has been disabled:

1. Locate the folder to share from the Desktop or by using Windows Explorer. To locate a folder in Windows Explorer, right-click Start, choose Explore All Users, expand Documents And Settings, look under your username, and locate the folder to share.

2. Right-click the folder and click Sharing And Security.

3. Select Share This Folder and create a share name, as shown in Figure 8-13. It's fine to leave User Limit: Maximum Allowed checked. The maximum is ten users.

FIGURE 8-13 Share the folder

4. Click Permissions. In the Permissions dialog box, shown in Figure 8-14, notice that the default group is Everyone (that means everyone on the network), and those users can change and read the data in the folder. To change that, select or deselect any entry.

5. In the same Permissions dialog box, you can add or remove groups of users or even specific users if you desire. Click Add to add a group or user, or click Remove to remove one. Although I advise against it for the beginner to intermediate user, or anyone not experienced with groups, you can remove the Everyone group and add a specific group of users or single users. For each group or user, you can apply permissions separately. If you want to go this route, read the Windows XP Help And Support files, and read through Chapter 11 in this book. Click OK.

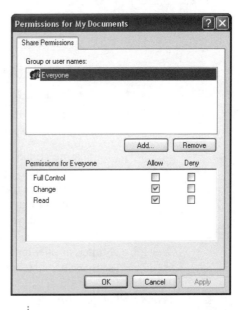

FIGURE 8-14 Setting share permissions

FIGURE 8-15 Configure advanced security

6. Back in the Properties dialog box, click the Security tab. Again, as with the previous steps, you can select a group or a user, and configure specific advanced permissions, as shown in Figure 8-15. You can also add or remove groups here. Again, this is quite tricky, and is only an option for advanced users and those who have read Chapter 10 and the Help And Support files. Click OK.

Although configuring and applying group permissions is simple—click Remove to remove the Everyone group and click Add to add a group you've created from your users (as detailed in Chapter 11)— it's quite a complicated issue. If a user belongs to a group with certain share permissions, and that group also has applied NTFS permissions, the "effective" permission for those users is difficult to calculate. In addition, if certain permissions are applied to the user individually, that complicates things too. If you're still interested, read up on the subject and consider taking a class or two!

◥ There's No Need for a Printer at Every Computer

Share printers and other hardware so they can be accessed from any computer on the network.

Sharing printers and other hardware is just as easy as sharing a folder. Once the printer is shared, any user can print to it from any computer on the network. This makes having multiple printers unnecessary. One printer will suffice (or maybe two if you have a specialty photo printer). Once the printer is shared, you can set permissions for it if you are using Windows XP Professional. You can let everyone have complete control over the printer, or only let users print, and deny access to print queues and other settings. It's up to you.

 The second part of this example assumes you have Simple File Sharing turned off and are using Windows XP Professional. Advanced permissions cannot be set for printers if Simple File Sharing is in use or if you are on Windows XP Home Edition.

To share a printer on either Windows XP Home or Professional:

1. Click Start | Printers And Faxes.

2. Right-click the printer to share, and choose Sharing.

3. In the printer's Properties dialog box, shown in Figure 8-16, click the Sharing tab and select Share This Printer. Type a name for the printer.

4. Click Additional Drivers.

5. In the Additional Drivers dialog box, check the drivers that apply. Choices are available for Windows 95, 98, and Me, Windows NT 4.0 or 2000, and Windows XP.

6. Click OK. Do not close the Properties dialog box.

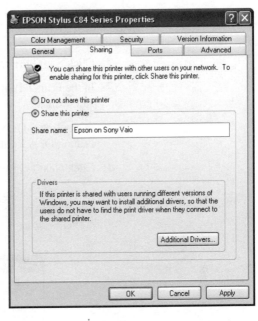

FIGURE 8-16   Sharing a printer

To set share permissions on Windows XP Professional machines:

1. In the printer Properties dialog box, click the Security tab. If you don't see a Security tab, you have Simple File Sharing enabled. To disable Simple File Sharing, read the previous section.

2. By default, everyone who has access to this computer can print to it. You can allow everyone to do more, though, including manage printers and documents if you desire. To add permissions, click Everyone, and check the items under Allow, as shown in Figure 8-17. Click OK when finished.

Denying permissions is done the same way, and you can add or remove groups from the Group Or User Names area. However, this is getting a little beyond our scope here. More information on shares and local users and groups is provided in Chapter 11.

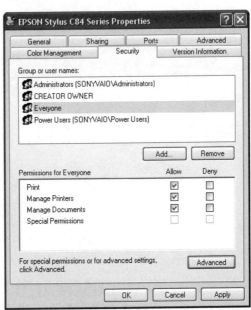

FIGURE 8-17   Adding permissions

8

Once the printer is shared, it must be set up at each of the networked computers:

1. Click Start | Printers And Faxes.

2. In the Printer Tasks pane, select Add A Printer. Click Next to start the Add Printer Wizard.

3. In the Local Or Network Printer dialog box, select A Network Printer, Or A Printer Attached To Another Computer. Click Next.

4. Click Next to browse for the printer.

5. Locate the shared printer in the list, and click Next. Figure 8-18 shows three computers, with one selected, which has two available printers.

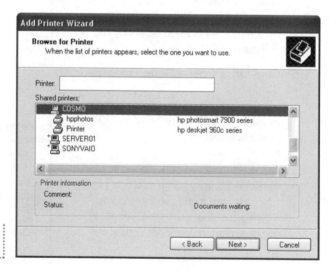

FIGURE 8-18 Browse to the shared printer

6. If prompted about installing a driver, click Yes.

7. When prompted to make this the default printer, click Yes or No, and then Next. Click Finish. The new printer will appear in the Printers And Faxes window.

TAKE COMMAND WITH COMMAND-LINE TOOLS

If you've set up the network and created shared folders, but find that you have problems connecting to specific computers on the network, there are some tools that you can use to help find solutions. Before using these tools, though, run the Network Setup Wizard on the host again, use the network setup disk on all of the other computers, and then double-check the physical connections. Make sure to verify that everything is plugged in and working properly, and that the lights are on for all NICs and hubs.

If all of that seems to be functioning, try the Network Diagnostics option in the Help And Support files, found under Pick A Task And Use Tools To View Your Computer Information And Diagnose Problems. If that doesn't help, you likely have some rather serious problems. To continue troubleshooting on your own, you can use the following command-line tools to see which computer is having trouble communicating with the others: `ipconfig /all` and `ping`.

⬎ Get Configuration Information with ipconfig /all

The `ipconfig /all` command lets you easily view a computer's connection information.

8

If you know a little about TCP/IP (Transmission Control Protocol/Internet Protocol), you know that computers communicate on a network and over the Internet by using specific numbers called IP addresses, and these addresses distinguish them from other computers on the network. IP addresses are created from four sets of numbers, one to three digits each, such as 192.168.0.5. Each computer on a network must be configured with an IP address that is different from every other on the network, the same way a computer must have a computer name that is distinct. If you've created a home network (workgroup) using the Network Setup Wizard, these IP addresses were created automatically.

When performing advanced troubleshooting, you'll want to verify that all IP addresses on the network have the same pattern of numbers. For instance, if the IP addresses of three of the four computers on the network take the form 192.168.0.*x*, where *x* represents a single-digit number, the other computer's IP address must also follow that form. Again, each IP address must be distinct, which means in this example that *x* must be unique for each address. While IP addresses are *similar but different*, subnet masks are all the same. A subnet mask tells the computers who is on their network, and who is not. A computer with a different subnet mask from the others will not be reachable. An example of a subnet mask is 255.255.255.0.

When computers on a network can't communicate, and you want to perform advanced troubleshooting, you can find out what IP address each computer has been assigned by using the `ipconfig /all` command. The information output by `ipconfig /all` may give you insight as to the problem. Figure 8-19 shows an example of the output. Notice the IP address and subnet mask for this computer.

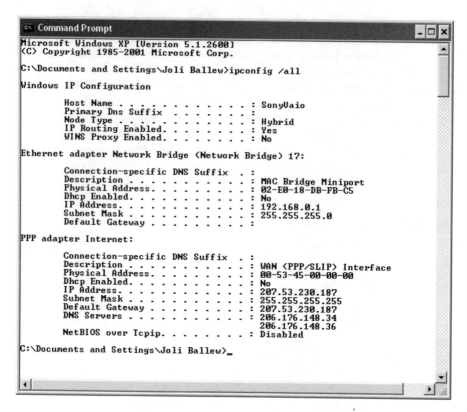

```
Command Prompt                                                    _ □ ×

Microsoft Windows XP [Version 5.1.2600]
(C) Copyright 1985-2001 Microsoft Corp.

C:\Documents and Settings\Joli Ballew>ipconfig /all

Windows IP Configuration

        Host Name . . . . . . . . . . . . : SonyVaio
        Primary Dns Suffix  . . . . . . . :
        Node Type . . . . . . . . . . . . : Hybrid
        IP Routing Enabled. . . . . . . . : Yes
        WINS Proxy Enabled. . . . . . . . : No

Ethernet adapter Network Bridge (Network Bridge) 17:

        Connection-specific DNS Suffix  . :
        Description . . . . . . . . . . . : MAC Bridge Miniport
        Physical Address. . . . . . . . . : 02-E0-18-DB-FB-C5
        Dhcp Enabled. . . . . . . . . . . : No
        IP Address. . . . . . . . . . . . : 192.168.0.1
        Subnet Mask . . . . . . . . . . . : 255.255.255.0
        Default Gateway . . . . . . . . . :

PPP adapter Internet:

        Connection-specific DNS Suffix  . :
        Description . . . . . . . . . . . : WAN (PPP/SLIP) Interface
        Physical Address. . . . . . . . . : 00-53-45-00-00-00
        Dhcp Enabled. . . . . . . . . . . : No
        IP Address. . . . . . . . . . . . : 207.53.230.187
        Subnet Mask . . . . . . . . . . . : 255.255.255.255
        Default Gateway . . . . . . . . . : 207.53.230.187
        DNS Servers . . . . . . . . . . . : 206.176.148.34
                                            206.176.148.36
        NetBIOS over Tcpip. . . . . . . . : Disabled

C:\Documents and Settings\Joli Ballew>_
```

FIGURE 8-19 The IP address and subnet mask are displayed by using ipconfig /all.

 This section assumes you've created a workgroup using the Network Setup Wizard. If you've created a workgroup (or a domain) in any other manner, the premise will be the same, but the IP addresses and subnet masks will differ.

To get this information and troubleshoot connectivity on the network, at each computer:

1. Click Start | All Programs | Accessories | Command Prompt.

2. At the command prompt, type **ipconfig /all**.

3. Locate the IP address for the local area connection, generally under Ethernet Adapter. Verify that the IP addresses are all similar, 192.168.0.*x*, where *x* is unique for each so that there are no duplicate addresses.

4. Locate the subnet mask for the local area connection, generally under Ethernet Adapter. Verify that the subnet mask for all computers is 255.255.255.0.

If you find a computer that does not have the correct IP address or subnet mask, you need to correct it. There are multiple ways to do this. One way is to run the Network Setup Wizard again. Another is to change the network settings in the Properties dialog box of My Computer:

1. At each computer, right-click My Computer, choose Properties, and click the Computer Name tab.

2. Note what each workgroup name is, and what each computer name is. On the computer that has been deemed the problem computer, click Change.

3. In the Computer Name Changes dialog box, shown in Figure 8-20, type in a new name for the computer if the name is not distinct on the network. Type in the correct workgroup name. Click OK.

FIGURE 8-20 Change the computer name and workgroup name on a problem computer

4. Click OK twice more, and then click Yes to restart the computer.

5. Verify that you can reach network resources. If you cannot, run the Network Setup Wizard again on all computers. This will most likely *not* be necessary.

⬃ Ping for Problems

The ping *command lets you easily find out what computers aren't connecting to the network.*

This section assumes you've completed the previous section, using ipconfig /all, and are still having problems. Even if you've decided that all IP addresses, subnet masks, and computer names are correct, you may still not be able to connect to a specific computer. If that's the case, there may be more complex problems, such as a crimped cable or failed NIC you have yet to identify. To see if a computer can be reached from others on the network, you can *ping* it.

Pinging a computer simply verifies it's reachable using its IP address alone. Of course, you first need to use the ipconfig /all command on each computer and note its IP address. With that done, from a computer that is successfully connected to the network, ping the problem computer:

1. Choose Start | All Programs | Accessories | Command Prompt.

2. At the command prompt, type **ping** *ip address*.

If the request "times out," as shown in Figure 8-21, the computer you are trying to reach is not physically connected to the network (assuming you've verified that the IP address, subnet mask, and computer name are all correct). Continue troubleshooting by replacing cables, the computer's NIC, and possibly the hub. Occasionally, a hub will continue to work even though one or more of its inputs are bad. You can learn more about troubleshooting a network from Windows Help and Support files. The Home and Small Office Network Troubleshooter walks you through the steps systematically.

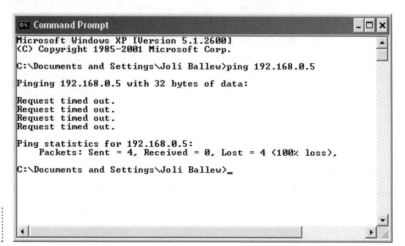

FIGURE 8-21 Bad connections time out.

Figure 8-22 shows a successful ping. This means the computer is physically connected to the network but has other issues. Rerun the Network Setup Wizard and recheck computer names, IP addresses, and subnet masks. Restart all computers.

```
Command Prompt                                           _ □ ×
Microsoft Windows XP [Version 5.1.2600]
(C) Copyright 1985-2001 Microsoft Corp.

C:\Documents and Settings\Joli Ballew>ping 192.168.0.68

Pinging 192.168.0.68 with 32 bytes of data:

Reply from 192.168.0.68: bytes=32 time<1ms TTL=128
Reply from 192.168.0.68: bytes=32 time<1ms TTL=128
Reply from 192.168.0.68: bytes=32 time<1ms TTL=128
Reply from 192.168.0.68: bytes=32 time<1ms TTL=128

Ping statistics for 192.168.0.68:
    Packets: Sent = 4, Received = 4, Lost = 0 (0% loss),
Approximate round trip times in milli-seconds:
    Minimum = 0ms, Maximum = 0ms, Average = 0ms

C:\Documents and Settings\Joli Ballew>_
```

FIGURE 8-22 Successful connections show results.

Now that your network is connected and working properly, it's time to get each computer running the absolute best it can. At every computer, you can enhance performance by getting rid of files and programs you don't need, disabling services you don't want, updating with Windows Update, and using tools that ship with Windows XP, including Disk Cleanup and Disk Defragmenter. Your computer can run faster and better with only a few simple tweaks, as discussed in the next chapter.

CHAPTER 9
IMPROVING SYSTEM PERFORMANCE

Improving the way your computer performs can be achieved in a variety of ways, but not always the way you think. You could, for instance, add a larger hard drive, surround-sound speakers, a microphone, or even a headphone. You can turn your computer into a fax machine. You can get a bigger monitor, get a flat screen, or even set up dual monitors by adding a second video card. You can even add a USB hub and connect every device you own simultaneously. However, none of those things makes your computer *run faster*. They just make it look better or make it more pleasurable to work with. If you want it to run better, you have to work from the inside out.

Adding more RAM is the easiest way to get a quick *performance* boost. You have to pay for that, though, and that's not the purpose of this chapter. (However, if you can afford it and you have the room, certainly go right ahead.) I want to show you how to increase performance without buying or installing anything. You can improve performance in just a few minutes by taking steps to get your computer back in top form.

In this chapter, you'll learn some of my favorite performance tricks. Those tricks include deleting unnecessary files and programs, getting rid of Windows components you don't use, updating old and problematic drivers, and scheduling important tasks. Some of the tasks you can schedule include using Disk Cleanup, Disk Defragmenter, and Automatic Updates.

CLEAN UP YOUR DRIVES

I'll bet you usually remember to clean your house occasionally. You do this cleaning so that your house doesn't begin to fall into ruin. It's a necessary part of life. Unfortunately, you might not remember to take the same care with your computer. However, it's just as important. A clean and well-organized computer will run faster, enable you to work faster, and have additional free hard drive space available when you need it. There are two things to get rid of: files and applications.

⬎ Rid Your Computer of Unnecessary Files

You have tons of files you don't need; delete them and free up some hard drive space.

Every time you create a document, copy a picture from your digital camera to your hard drive, download a music file, open and save an attachment in an e-mail, create a graphic, import video and create a movie, or work on a project, you're saving data and files to your hard drive.

These files accumulate, and if you never delete the files you no longer need, you're probably wasting quite a bit of hard drive space. Not only that, but the computer must sift through all of these files when searching for data. Unnecessary files and data slow down the computer and take up valuable space on the hard drive.

Every now and then you should go through these files and delete what you no longer want. It's a simple task, but one that takes time. Figure 9-1 shows an example of some unnecessary files in the My Documents folder on my hard disk.

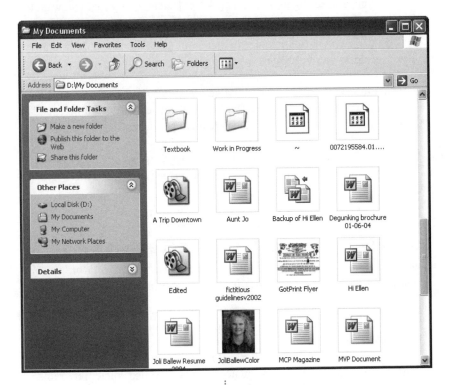

FIGURE 9-1 You almost always have files that you can delete.

Getting rid of unnecessary files, no matter what they contain, is simple:

1. Click Start | My Computer.

2. Select the disk where data is stored. If there is only one choice, it is probably C:. If two or more choices are available, try D: or E:.

3. Open the My Documents folder first. Locate any file you no longer need, right-click it, and click Delete. Verify that you want to perform this action by clicking Yes when prompted. You can also delete a selected folder by pressing DEL on your keyboard.

4. Click the Back button and select My Pictures. Locate any file you no longer need, right-click it, and click Delete. Verify that you want to perform this action by clicking Yes when prompted.

5. Click the Back button and select My Movies. Locate any file you no longer need, right-click it, and select Delete. Verify that you want to perform this action by clicking Yes when prompted.

6. Continue in this manner to clean out My Videos and data in any folders you've created.

In a few days, after you're positive you don't need anything you've deleted, empty the Recycle Bin. The files you deleted will be in there, and thus on your hard drive, until you delete them permanently.

 Even though deleting unnecessary files is a straightforward task, it is one often overlooked. Perform this task whenever you feel it's necessary. For some this may be once a month, for others, once a year.

⬋ Rid Your Computer of Unnecessary Programs

You have tons of programs you don't need, and some you don't even know you have; remove them for more power and hard drive space.

Okay, getting rid of unnecessary files may have seemed a little obvious, but I had to mention it because most people never do it. They just collect and collect and collect until the hard drive is so full that the computer owner figures the only way out is to purchase a new computer. People collect stuff besides the data that they create, though; they also collect programs and applications. Take a look at Figure 9-2; there are lots of unnecessary programs here, as indicated by the Rarely label, a sign that the program is not needed and can likely be uninstalled.

To see what programs are installed on your computer that you use rarely:

1. Open Control Panel from the Start menu or from the Desktop.

2. Open Add Or Remove Programs.

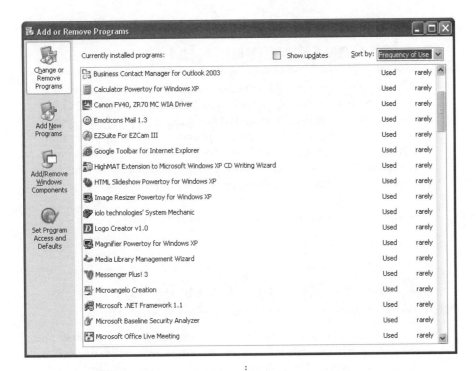

FIGURE 9-2 Most people store unnecessary applications.

3. In the Add Or Remove Programs window, in the Sort By drop-down list, choose Frequency Of Use.

4. Take a look at all of the programs that are used "Rarely." Decide what you can remove. A good rule of thumb is the one-year rule. If you haven't used the program in a year, delete it. To every rule of thumb there's an exception, so be sure you don't kill a program you rarely use but may need later.

To remove any program in the list, click Change/Remove. Follow the prompts to remove the program. Once you've deleted everything you need to, use Disk Cleanup and Disk Defragmenter, as detailed later in this chapter, to help reorganize the items still stored on your hard disk.

CLOSE OPEN WINDOWS (APPLICATION WINDOWS THAT IS)

Windows XP ships with all kinds of applications, services, and components that you may or may not need. Some, like System Restore and Windows Update, are important to manage and run because they keep the system secure. However, some, such as Fax Services, MSN Explorer, and Networking Services, may not be necessary or required by you or your computer. Unnecessary items can be disabled, uninstalled, or otherwise immobilized so that they don't use up hard drive space or system resources.

 Remember, the less your computer has to do, the faster it will perform.

⬐ Get the Most from System Restore

System Restore won't help you much if you don't use it.

System Restore can be used to restore your computer to an earlier time if it ever becomes unstable. Restoring the system to an earlier time will not cause loss of personal data, though, meaning you won't lose any documents, photos, movies, music, e-mail, or even Internet Favorites. System Restore creates *restore points* automatically, and if problems ever do occur, you won't have to reinstall the operating system to recover. System Restore can be used to recover from problematic application or driver installations, as well as partial downloads that cause a computer to hang or fail.

System Restore can be accessed from Start | All Programs | Accessories | System Tools | System Restore. The interface is shown in Figure 9-3. Clicking System Restore Settings in the left pane brings up the settings, shown in Figure 9-4. In this, there are two drives, C: and D:—you may only see one drive, or you may see more than two.

Because System Restore is such a powerful tool, consider these additional tweaks to make sure it works to its potential and is available and functional when and if you need it:

- Always leave Turn Off System Restore On All Drives unchecked.

- Make sure all drives are monitored and that their status is denoted as Monitoring.

- For each drive, select the drive and click Settings. The Disk Space To Use settings should be set to approximately 1GB (or 1000MB).

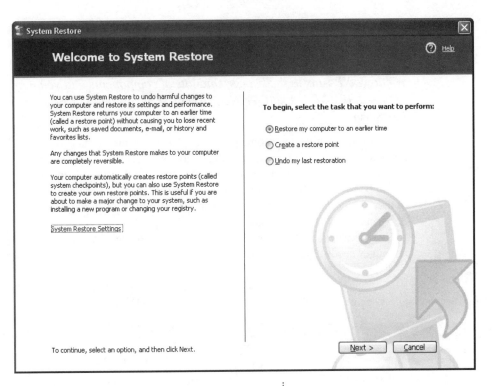

FIGURE 9-3 System Restore can be a life saver.

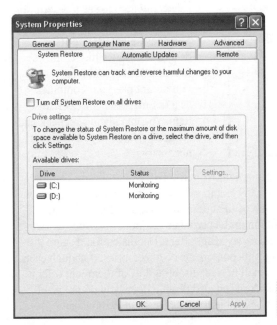

FIGURE 9-4 Configure System Restore Properties for best results.

↘ Remove Fax Services and Other Windows Components

Windows XP runs in the background lots of components that you may not need, like MSN Explorer, Networking Services, and maybe even Fax Services.

Now that you've done some pretty easy housecleaning tasks, you are ready to move on to a few tasks that may not be so evident. You may have Windows applications and services installed that you don't need, and it would be to your advantage to uninstall or disable them. I introduced some of these in Chapter 2, but many others may be disabled, including Fax Services, MSN Messenger, and more.

To see what's installed on your computer, and to decide what you may no longer need:

FIGURE 9-5 Several services can be uninstalled.

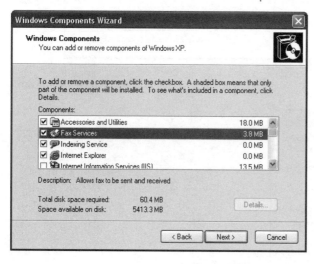

1. Choose Start | Control Panel and click Add Or Remove Programs.

2. In the Add Or Remove Programs window, click Add/Remove Windows Components.

3. Scroll through the Components list, shown in Figure 9-5, and select any item to see a description of it. This figure shows Fax Services selected, and its description states that it allows faxes to be sent and received. If you do not use your computer as a fax machine, uncheck this item. You can always recheck and reinstall it later, if you decide it's necessary.

4. Select another component from the list. Some offer a Details button, which you can click to see more information. Accessories And Utilities is one of the components that offers a Details button. This component has two subcomponents: Accessories and Games. Both choices again offer a Details button. Figure 9-6 shows the optional subcomponents of Accessories. Although each subcomponent is small in size, disabling lots of them will offer a performance boost. You can also disable items you do not want other users to have available, such as Desktop Wallpaper.

5. Consider disabling or uninstalling the following if you do not need them, and click Next when finished:

■ Indexing Service

■ Internet Information Services

■ MSN Explorer

■ Other Network File And Print Services

■ Windows Media Player

■ Windows Messenger

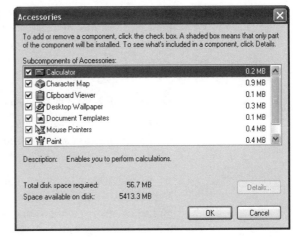

FIGURE 9-6 Disable subcomponents

UPDATE DRIVERS

Now that you've cleaned up a little bit, let's talk about drivers. Drivers are the software that enables your hardware to communicate with your computer, and vice versa. Without the appropriate drivers, you won't be able to scan, print, download pictures from your digital camera, communicate with your web cam, or even use your wireless mouse. When you get a new computer and install your peripherals, you also install their drivers. Usually, Windows XP knows what drivers to install and does so automatically, but sometimes you have to install the driver from a disk that came with the hardware.

When particular hardware is not on Microsoft's Hardware Compatibility List (HCL), its drivers are not "signed." Signed drivers have been thoroughly tested by Microsoft and have proven to work properly with Windows XP. If a driver is not signed, you'll likely have difficulties related to it. The computer may "blue screen," a situation where the computer completely crashes and all you see is a blue screen with some gibberish written on it, the hardware may not work properly, or the computer may simply "act up." Many times, these problems occur even when you are not using the device. When this happens, it's extremely difficult to locate the problem.

The solution to such problems is to always keep your drivers updated and keep an eye out for problems (and when they happen). Make sure all of your hardware is on Microsoft's HCL too. Staying updated may entail downloading driver updates from the Windows Update web site, obtaining them from the manufacturer, or even purchasing them. Updated drivers keep your computer in the best shape possible, not only by helping the hardware and computer communicate effectively, but by also offering more security, improved features, and enhanced performance. When problems occur with drivers, use Event Viewer to search for answers.

⬰ Event Viewer Can Tell You What's Wrong

Event Viewer is an application that gathers information about the hardware and software on your computer and logs errors and problems; you can use the logs as troubleshooting tools.

Event Viewer, an application that is part of Windows XP, both Home and Professional, logs significant events automatically. You can view the logged events to troubleshoot problems with hardware, software, and the operating system. The events recorded have to do with three things: applications, security, and the system itself. Event Viewer uses this information to create three logs: Application, Security, and System.

- **Application log**   Offers information about potential problems with applications, such as errors reading from program files or problems obtaining updates for antivirus software.

- **Security log**   Offers information about events regarding invalid logon attempts and creating, opening, and deleting files, all of which may be potential security threats.

- **System log**   Offers information about drivers and system components, such as failed drivers, failures of hardware, or bad blocks of memory.

Each log contains three types of entries: Error, Warning, and Information. Errors are significant problems, those that can cause data loss, such as driver failures or memory or hard drive problems. Warnings are not as problematic, but may indicate possible future problems. Information entries are events that describe successful events, such as the successful loading of a driver on bootup.

To see what problems, if any, exist on your computer, you'll want to peruse these logs occasionally. System logs offer the most information about drivers, and thus are a good place to start. However, in the name of keeping the computer secure, you should also get used to looking over the Security logs occasionally as well. To see if any problems exist with drivers on your computer:

1. Choose Start | Search and, in the Search box, type **Administrative Tools**.

2. Open the Administrative Tools folder and click Event Viewer. This is shown in Figure 9-7.

FIGURE 9-7   Locate Event Viewer in Administrative Tools

3. Select System, click the Type column heading in the right pane, and locate the errors. An example is shown in Figure 9-8.

4. The Source listing gives a hint to the problem. Double-click any error listing to see an explanation. Figure 9-9 shows an example of a problem with a printer driver. This particular problem has to do with the Epson Stylus C-84 printer installed on this computer. The Power Driver is unknown, and the suggestion is to reinstall the driver. There's also a link for more information.

5. Click the link offered to obtain more information. Click Yes to send the information over the Internet.

6. If you're lucky, you'll be offered more information on solving the problem. This isn't always the case, though.

7. Reinstall the driver for the problem device or use Windows Update to see if a new one is available. You should also check the manufacturer's web site for information related to the problem.

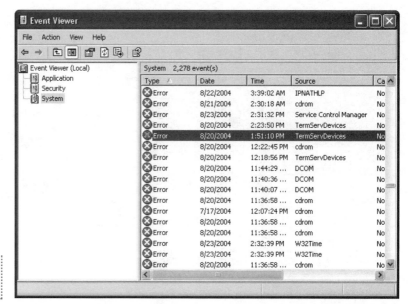

FIGURE 9-8　Locate errors in Event Viewer

FIGURE 9-9　Event Viewer details problems and offers solutions.

You can learn quite a bit from Event Viewer's logs. Note, however, that the default size for each log is 512KB, and when that is reached, newer events start overwriting older ones. For that reason, you should check the logs weekly. You also can increase the size of the log:

1. In Event Viewer, right-click the log to change and click Properties.

2. In the System Properties dialog box for the log, under Log Size, type in a larger log size.

3. Click OK.

⬎ Find Any Driver on the Web

Drivers should be as current as possible, and there are lots of places on the Web to find updated ones.

Drivers that are not signed and drivers that are not up-to-date are dangerous pieces of software. Unruly drivers can cause your hardware or software to hang, cause your printer to print garbled text, and even cause your computer to crash. If you want to enhance system performance, you need to make a concerted effort to keep your drivers updated. There are several ways to do this, listed next in order from most trusted to least:

- Windows Update
- Manufacturer's web site
- CD-ROM that came with the hardware
- Well-known third-party web sites such as **http://www.windrivers.com**
- Message boards and lesser-known third-party web sites

Of course, if a driver is offered to you via Windows Update, it's been signed and can be installed safely. Manufacturers offer their drivers too, and although these are almost always okay to install, they may not be signed. CD-ROMs that come with your hardware are a good choice too, but they typically are older than what the manufacturer offers on the web site.

If the previous three options don't offer new drivers, and if your computer is having problems with an existing driver, you can try well-known third-party web sites such as WinDriver.com, DriverGuide.com, and PCDrivers.com. On these sites, you can view drivers that may have been created for another piece of hardware but that have been tested and proven to work on others. Users write comments about each driver, offering a personal touch. Finally, drivers can be obtained from other sites, such as message boards and lesser-known third-party web sites, but this should be a last resort.

⬎ Use Device Driver Rollback

If you try a driver for a hardware device and it doesn't work as expected, use Device Driver Rollback to revert to the previous driver.

When you install a new driver, Windows XP automatically creates a backup of the old driver for you, just in case things go awry. When used, Device Driver Rollback reverts your computer to the original driver you were using before the change. To use Device Driver Rollback, you must first locate the hardware in Device Manager.

To locate the driver in Device Manager and use Device Driver Rollback:

1. Right-click My Computer and click Properties.

2. On the Hardware tab, click Device Manager.

3. In the Device Manager window, locate the problem device. Sometimes the device that isn't working properly will have a red X by it, as shown in Figure 9-10, sometimes a yellow exclamation point, and other times nothing.

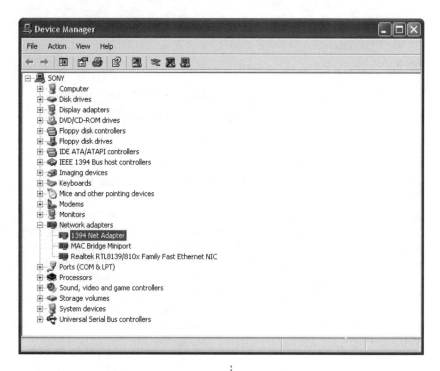

FIGURE 9-10 This network adapter is not functioning correctly.

4. Double-click the problem device and choose the Driver tab, shown in Figure 9-11.

5. Click Roll Back Driver. Click OK when finished.

If your device isn't listed in Device Manager, which is the case with printers, scanners, and digital cameras, you can use System Restore to roll back the driver. Using System Restore is generally the best choice. However, you can also work through the Help and Support troubleshooting wizards. To access the wizards:

1. Click Start | Help And Support.

2. Under Pick A Help Topic, click Fixing A Problem.

3. Under Fixing A Problem, select a wizard. Available wizards include Printing Problems and Hardware And System Device Problems.

4. In the right pane, click the troubleshooter and work through it.

FIGURE 9-11 Device Driver Rollback is under the Driver tab.

OPTIMIZE THE HARD DISK ON A SCHEDULE

Now that you've done a little cleaning and have your drivers updated, it's time to take a look at the hard disk. The hard disk is the piece of hardware you save data to, and it is responsible for holding all of the data you accumulate. Therefore, it's extremely important to take care of it. You should regularly use Disk Cleanup to get rid of unnecessary and temporary files created by the OS, use Disk Defragmenter to keep contiguous files together, keep antivirus software up to date, and stay on top of Windows Updates. If you find all of this difficult to remember, you should configure these things to run on a schedule. That's exactly what you'll learn here. Using Scheduled Tasks in Control Panel, you can schedule almost anything, and either have tasks run automatically (perhaps while you sleep) or be reminded by Scheduled Tasks to run them when you're at the computer.

Schedule Disk Cleanup

Schedule Disk Cleanup and you won't ever forget to run it again.

Disk Cleanup is an application accessible in System Tools that helps you rid your computer of unnecessary files. Unnecessary files take up hard drive space and may cause your computer to perform sluggishly. Unnecessary files you can delete using Disk Cleanup include the following (you may or may not have all of these):

- **Downloaded program files**   Files automatically downloaded to your computer when you view certain web pages on the Internet. These are usually Java applets and ActiveX controls and are temporary.

- **Temporary Internet files**   Web pages you've visited that are temporarily saved to your hard disk. When revisiting a page, some of the content is pulled from these files, which makes accessing previously viewed web pages faster.

- **Old Chkdsk files**   File fragments found and saved by Chkdsk.

- **Offline web pages**   Web pages you decide to store on your computer so that you can view them later, when you're offline.

- **Microsoft Office temporary files**   Log files for Microsoft Office used for diagnostic purposes.

- **Microsoft Office Error Reporting temporary files**   Files that are temporarily saved for reporting to Microsoft errors that have occurred.

- **Office setup files**   Installation files used by Microsoft Office. It is recommended you do not delete these files unless you can easily access the Microsoft Office CD-ROMs when needed.

- **Recycle Bin files**   Files you have previously deleted from your computer.

- **Temporary files**   Files created by third-party applications for use during the operation of that program. These are generally deleted when the program exits, but not always.

- **WebClient/Publisher temporary files**   A cache of files previously accessed on the hard disk. They are used to increase performance.

Because Disk Cleanup is such a valuable tool, and because many people fail to run it on a regular basis, it's best to schedule Disk Cleanup to run on a daily or weekly basis automatically. This can be done in Control Panel, using Scheduled Tasks. Before configuring it to run in Scheduled Tasks, though, you have to run Disk Cleanup once to configure the parameters with which it will run in the future. The following steps explain how.

1. Choose Start | All Programs | Accessories | System Tools | Disk Cleanup.

2. If multiple drives exist, you are prompted to select a drive to clean up. Select the drive and click OK.

3. Check the items you want to delete, similar to the example shown in Figure 9-12. Click OK when finished. Click Yes to verify that you want to perform these actions.

FIGURE 9-12   Select the items to delete

 Disk Cleanup also offers an option to compress old catalog files created by the Indexing Service. Compressing files you don't use often will save disk space. If you use the Indexing Service, check this box.

Next, you have to make sure that a password is assigned to an administrator who accesses the computer—the one who will configure Disk Cleanup—so that Disk Cleanup can verify that it has permission before running:

1. Open Control Panel, and open User Accounts.

2. Verify that at least one administrator account requires a password. If one does, you'll see Password Protected under the account. If none does, you must configure one.

3. To configure a password, click Change An Account and select an account to change.

4. Click Create A Password.

5. Type and retype the new password. Click Create Password.

Figure 9-13 shows four accounts. Joli Ballew is a computer administrator, and her account is password protected. Cosmo is a limited user, and her account is password protected. The Administrator account is password protected, and the Guest account is off. Either computer administrator account can be used to configure Scheduled Tasks.

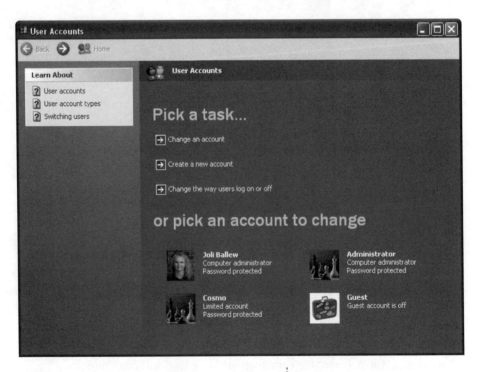

FIGURE 9-13 Password protect at least one administrator account

Once you've configured Disk Cleanup with the proper parameters and have a password-protected administrator account, you can run Scheduled Tasks and configure Disk Cleanup to run automatically:

1. Choose Start | Control Panel. If in Category view, click Performance And Maintenance and then choose Scheduled Tasks.

2. In the Scheduled Tasks window, click Add Scheduled Task. The Scheduled Task Wizard will open; click Next to start the wizard.

3. When prompted, as shown in Figure 9-14, scroll down to Disk Cleanup, select it, and click Next.

4. Name the task **Disk Cleanup**, and specify how often to perform the task. Once a week is fine. Click Next.

5. Choose a start time, state when to perform the task, and specify a start date. Click Next.

6. Enter and confirm the password for your account. Click Next.

7. Choose Open Advanced Properties For This Task When I Click Finish, and then click Finish.

FIGURE 9-14 Configure Disk Cleanup as a Scheduled Task

8. Verify that the schedule and other properties are correct, and make changes as necessary. Make sure the task is enabled (check Enabled), and view the options under the Settings tab. Click OK.

The task will now run on a schedule and keep your computer clean automatically.

Schedule Disk Defragmenter
Your hard drives should be defragmented a couple of times a year.

When a file that is written to the hard disk is deleted, it leaves a gap of available space on the hard disk. The next file that is written to the disk is saved to the first open spot on the disk, which may be the gap left by the deleted file. If the new file does not fit completely in the gap, the part that fits is stored in the gap and the remaining fragment is stored in the next open spot. The file may be fragmented into many chunks, if necessary, to fit in open gaps. When the hard disk has to locate all the parts of a fragmented file before displaying it, the file takes longer to display than it would if the file were not fragmented. This decreases the computer's performance and slows its response to user requests. Disk Defragmenter is an application that reorders file fragments so that complete files are stored contiguously on the disk, which improve the computer's performance and responsiveness.

Because of the importance of keeping files together, it's important to run Disk Defragmenter a few times a year (or more). As with Disk Cleanup, you can use Scheduled Tasks to remind you when it's time to do this. By default, you can't schedule Disk Defragmenter, and it isn't listed as an option, so you have to cheat the system a little and use the nifty trick I'll show you here.

To trick Scheduled Tasks into running Disk Defragmenter:

1. Open Control Panel and then open Scheduled Tasks. (If you're using Category view, click Performance And Maintenance first.)

2. Click Add Scheduled Task. Click Next to start the wizard.

3. Disk Defragmenter will not be available in the Application list (shown earlier in Figure 9-14). Click Browse.

4. On the root drive, generally C:, browse to Windows | System32 | defrag.exe, as shown in Figure 9-15. Do not choose dfrg.msc. (You may or may not see the filename extensions.) Click Open.

FIGURE 9-15 Locate the Disk Defragmenter executable file

5. Name the task **Disk Defragmenter**, and select Monthly. Click Next.

6. Choose a start time (e.g., at night just before you go to bed), and select two to four months of the year. Select the day of the month to run the task. Figure 9-16 shows a workable schedule. Click Next.

7. Enter and confirm the password for your account. Click Next.

8. Select Open Advanced Properties For This Task When I Click Finish, and then click Finish.

9. Verify that the schedule and other properties are correct, and make changes as necessary. Make sure the task is enabled (check Enabled), and view the options under the Settings tab. Click OK.

The task will now run on this schedule and defragment your drive automatically.

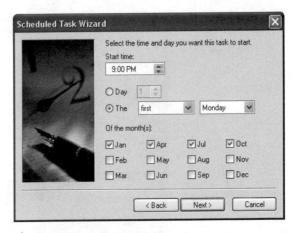

FIGURE 9-16 Configure Disk Defragmenter to run a few times a year

Schedule Antivirus Software Updates

Schedule antivirus software to get updates and run scans to make sure you're always protected.

With your computer now set to automatically perform tasks, it's time to configure your antivirus software to do the same. For the most part, this is done inside the antivirus software itself, and you configure it when you install the application. If you have a "full service" package, one that also lets you scan for Windows problems, optimize performance, and perform system maintenance tasks, you may want to configure those to run on a schedule too. It can't hurt to scan your system and find and fix errors once a month.

Figure 9-17 shows the tasks scheduled for a sample computer. Disk Cleanup and Disk Defragmenter are configured, as are two Norton AntiVirus tasks. In addition, Outlook Express is configured to run every time the computer boots up. If you don't see these in your Scheduled Tasks folder, your antivirus or optimization software isn't scheduled to run as it should.

To configure Scheduled Tasks to run antivirus or optimization software on a schedule:

1. Open Control Panel and then open Scheduled Tasks. (If you're using Category view, click Performance And Maintenance first.)

2. Click Add Scheduled Task. Click Next to start the wizard.

FIGURE 9-17   Antivirus software should run on a schedule.

3. Under Application, locate the program to run. Figure 9-18 shows Norton WinDoctor. Click Next.

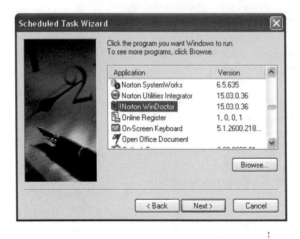

FIGURE 9-18   Locate the antivirus or optimization software to run

4. Name the task, and select how often to perform it. Click Next.

5. Choose a start time, and select when to run the task. Click Next.

6. Enter and confirm the password for your account. Click Next.

7. Select Open Advanced Properties For This Task When I Click Finish, and then click Finish.

8. Verify that the schedule and other properties are correct, and make changes as necessary. Make sure the task is enabled (check Enabled), and view the options under the Settings tab. Click OK.

The task will now run on this schedule, using the parameters set for it the last time you ran it.

⬂ Schedule Windows Updates

There are several ways to schedule Windows Updates, including through Scheduled Tasks or from System Properties.

Windows Update, introduced briefly in Chapter 5, is an automatic service that can be used to keep your computer configured with the latest Microsoft service packs and updates. If Automatic Updates is enabled, your computer will automatically download the recommended updates and install them, at a time convenient for you. You can also configure the service to download updates but not install them until you're ready; configure the service to only notify you when updates are available; or disable the service completely.

It has been my experience that configuring Automatic Updates to download updates when they are available and install them automatically works best for most people. These updates need to be installed, because they repair problems and glitches with the operating system, plug security holes in Internet Explorer and Outlook Express, and even introduce new Control Panel icons and options, as is true for Service Pack 2. Configuring this to happen automatically reduces the chances you'll forget to do it entirely.

 Not all users need all updates. If you consider yourself a power user, you may want to look over each update before it's installed. If that's the case, from the Automatic Updates tab, choose Download Updates For Me, But Let Me Choose When To Install Them.

However, if you need all the computing power you can get when you're working or gaming or connected to the Internet, configuring the updates to download and install at night (or some other idle time) may be a better option. If you want total control over what is downloaded and installed on your computer, then choose to have Automatic Updates notify you of updates, but never download or install them. That way, you can decide which updates you want to download and install. All of these are options in System Properties.

As mentioned, there are several ways to get the required updates:

- Visit **http://www.windowsupdate.com** and manually look for operating system and driver updates

- Configure Automatic Updates in System Properties to meet specific criteria

- Configure Automatic Updates to run using Scheduled Tasks

Getting updates from the web site was detailed in Chapter 5, so here I'll discuss the other two options.

To configure System Properties to acquire Automatic Updates using the criteria you specify:

1. Open Control Panel and then open System. If you're in Category view, choose Performance And Maintenance and then open System.

2. In System Properties, click the Automatic Updates tab. If you installed Service Pack 2 as recommended in Chapter 5, you'll see what's shown in Figure 9-19. (If you haven't gotten SP2 yet, you'll have the same features for the most part, but the interface will be different.)

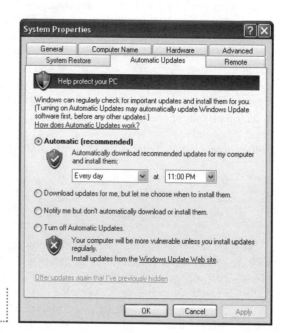

FIGURE 9-19 Automatic Updates is located in System Properties.

3. There are four choices, as detailed earlier in this section. Select the choice that best suits your needs, and configure a day and time if required. The setup in Figure 9-19 is the best option.

4. Click OK when finished.

 System Properties only allows you to schedule automatic downloads every day or once a week. To create a different type of schedule, use Scheduled Tasks.

To configure Automatic Updates as a Scheduled Task:

1. Open Control Panel and then open Scheduled Tasks. (If you're using Category view, click Performance And Maintenance first.)

2. Click Add Scheduled Task. Click Next to start the wizard.

3. Under Application, select Windows Updates. Click Next.

4. Choose when to perform the task. As with System Properties, you can choose to perform the task daily or weekly. Unlike System Properties, you can choose to run the task monthly, one time only, each time the computer starts, or each time you log on. Figure 9-20 shows the options. Click Next.

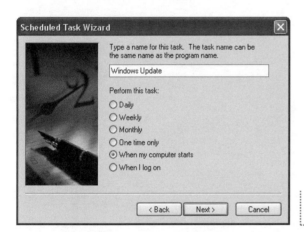

FIGURE 9-20 Scheduled Tasks offers more options for acquiring updates.

5. If applicable, choose a start time, and select when to run the task. (This won't be an option if you chose to run the task when the computer starts or when you log on.) Click Next.

6. Enter and confirm the password for your account. Click Next.

7. Select Open Advanced Properties For This Task When I Click Finish, and then click Finish.

8. Verify that the schedule and other properties are correct, and make changes as necessary. Make sure the task is enabled (check Enabled), and view the options under the Settings tab. Click OK.

The task will now run on this schedule, using the parameters set for it the last time you ran it.

Now that you have your computer in tip-top shape and running efficiently, and have tasks scheduled to run automatically, it's time to take even more control. In the next chapter, you'll learn how to do more than just improve system performance; you'll learn how to improve media performance. All of the topics in the next chapter are designed to be fun and useful—personalizing Windows Media Player, editing metafile data, creating a mobile picture library, commanding Media Player with your voice, and more. Stay tuned!

CHAPTER 10
MEDIA PERFORMANCE AND FUN

Now that you've improved system performance, networked all of your computers, and done quite a few things I consider *work*, you should take a few minutes to have a little fun with media. Windows XP offers lots of opportunities to work with media, including applications for working with photography, music, and video.

In this chapter you'll learn both how to enhance media application performance and how to get more from your own individual pieces of media. For photo buffs, you'll learn how to resize photos more efficiently, create slideshows for CDs, and create a video library you can take with you anywhere. Music and video buffs will discover how to edit Windows Media Player's metadata and how to personalize the Media Player. For all media users, I'll show you how to get the best media performance possible from the Media Player, how to secure it, and how to back up all of your media.

PHOTOGRAPHY

Getting started with digital photography usually means filling your hard drive with photos from your digital camera. Following that, there's generally some editing, perhaps some e-mailing, some printing of photos, and maybe even using your images as desktop backgrounds. You can do a lot more, though, and this section explores some of the options, including new and efficient ways to resize your images to make them easier to transmit and store; how to create slideshows you can burn to a CD and open on any computer; and how to create a mobile video picture library for your handheld PC or other mobile device.

 This section assumes that you know how to download and install software from the Internet, and that you have previous experience with digital pictures and the My Picture folder options.

◥ Resize Images Easily

Use the free Image Resizer PowerToy to resize images on the fly, without the hassle of opening them first.

Most people configure their digital cameras to take pictures using the highest quality possible. While this does indeed produce a better image, it also produces a large file. The large file size can become a problem when images need to be e-mailed or displayed on a web site (the transfer over phone or cable lines takes too long), archived to CDs (large files take up too much room), or used in an image-editing program (unnecessarily large files bog down image-editing programs).

You can resize images in almost any image-editing program by opening the program and changing the file's properties or attributes. In Microsoft Paint, for instance, you can open the image, click Image | Attributes, and, in the Attributes dialog box, type in the new width and height and state whether those dimensions are in inches, centimeters, or pixels. Other programs offer similar options. This procedure is inconvenient, though, because you have to open each image separately, and the entire process could take two or three minutes (or more) per picture. If you need to resize several images, perhaps all 100 recently downloaded from your digital camera, the process could end up an all-day chore.

There's an easier way. The Image Resizer PowerToy, available from **http://www.microsoft.com/windowsxp/pro/downloads/powertoys.asp**, allows you to resize single images without opening them, and is extremely easy to download, install, and use. It takes less than five minutes to download over a dial-up connection, and installs virtually by itself. Once installed, it allows you to resize images with a few clicks instead of several, and you won't even have to open the image.

To use the Image Resizer PowerToy once installed (remember, it's free):

1. Locate the picture or pictures to resize on your hard drive. They may be in My Pictures, or in some other folder you've created.

2. Select one or more pictures. To select noncontiguous pictures, hold down the CTRL key; to select contiguous pictures, hold down the SHIFT key.

3. Right-click the image(s). Click the new entry in the context menu, Resize Pictures.

4. In the Resize Pictures dialog box, shown in Figure 10-1, select the new image size and click Advanced. In the Advanced options, decide whether you want to make a copy of the image or resize the original picture. To resize the original, select Resize The Original Pictures (Don't Create Copies). To make a copy of the image and resize only that copy, check that box. Click OK.

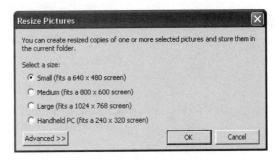

FIGURE 10-1 Choose the file size

The images will be resized automatically, and if copies were created, they will appear in the same folder as the originals. Otherwise, the original images will be resized.

◥ Create Slideshows Anyone Can Watch

Create a slideshow and burn it to a CD; anyone, even a Windows 95
user, will be able to watch it (and it will almost always open
automatically, too).

Slideshows aren't what they used to be; you no longer have to drag out
the projector and the slides, that's for sure. You can watch a slideshow quite
easily on your computer using the options available in Windows XP's My
Pictures folder or using Windows Picture and Fax Viewer. Unfortunately,
you can't distribute your favorite slideshows to others quite as effortlessly.
They're too big for e-mail, and if you burn them to a CD, there's no
guarantee your viewers will know what to do to view it as the slideshow
you intended. Thus, sharing your favorite slideshow requires a little more
thought, and one extra piece of free software.

The CD Slide Show Generator PowerToy, available at **http://www**
.microsoft.com/windowsxp/pro/downloads/powertoys.asp, adds an option
to Windows XP CD Writing Wizard to create a slideshow of the images
burned on the CD. You can run the slideshow on Windows 2000, Windows
NT, Windows Me, and Windows 9*x* systems. For the most part, the CD is
automatically played when the user places the CD in the CD-ROM drive as
well. As with the Image Resizer PowerToy, the download and installation is
quick and painless.

Once this PowerToy is installed, it's easy to create a CD that anyone can
watch, one that contains your favorite images in a slideshow:

1. Open the folder that contains the pictures you want to include in
   your slideshow, and verify that they are in the order in which you
   want them to appear. You can move pictures into a new order by
   dragging and dropping.

2. Choose Edit | Select All, and then Edit | Copy to copy the images.

3. Place a CD-R or CD-RW into the appropriate drive.

4. Open My Computer and the CD-R or CD-RW drive and click Edit |
   Paste. Make sure you are only copying pictures, though—the
   slideshow won't know what to do with Word documents.

5. In the CD Writing Tasks pane, shown in Figure 10-2, click Write
   These Files To CD.

6. When the CD Writing Wizard opens, type a name for the CD and
   click Next.

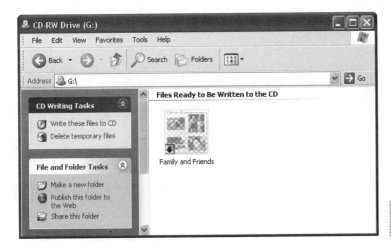

FIGURE 10-2 Write files to the CD

7. Work through the CD Writing Wizard. Options may differ here depending on other software installed on your system. A few pages in, you'll see a "Do You Want to Make A Picture CD?" page that's inserted by the CD Slide Show Generator PowerToy, with options to include the picture viewer or to write the CD normally. Choose Yes, Add A Picture Viewer and click Next.

You can now share this CD with anyone who owns practically any PC, no matter what Windows operating system it uses. The CD will automatically start and the pictures will be automatically displayed as a slideshow.

◥ Create a Mobile Picture Library

Use your digital photos, Movie Maker 2, and your Pocket PC or desktop PC to create a video photomontage that you can share.

When people ask to see photos of your kids, don't just open your wallet and flash a few photos; that's so *been-there-done-that*. Instead, turn on your Pocket PC and show them a video montage of your family. If you know how, you can even add music and narration. All you need are Windows XP, Movie Maker 2, and your own Pocket PC.

If you don't have a Pocket PC, you can still share your photomontage easily. As detailed in this section, you can save the photomontage to your hard drive and then e-mail it or burn it to a CD. Either way, it's a great way to share photos.

 It's helpful to have some knowledge of Movie Maker 2 before starting this project.

There are a few things to acquire and to do before you start:

- Decide what images you want to use from your digital photo library and in what order you want to add them. Put all images into a single folder by dragging and dropping.

- If you want to play a song as background for your photomontage, copy the song to the hard drive.

- If you plan to narrate your photomontage, connect and install a microphone.

- If you want to use special effects, title pages, credit pages, etc., in Movie Maker 2, acquire or create them.

When all of the items are available on your hard drive and you're ready to create your photomontage:

1. Choose Start | All Programs | Accessories | Windows Movie Maker. Make sure the Task Pane is accessible by clicking View | Taskpane.

2. In the Movie Tasks pane, under Capture Video, click Import Pictures.

3. In the Import File window, locate and select the images to import. Remember, you can select multiple noncontiguous pictures or contiguous pictures by holding down the CTRL key or SHIFT key, respectively. Click Import once the images have been selected. The images will appear in the Collections pane of Movie Maker 2, shown in Figure 10-3.

4. Select the first image in the Collections pane and choose Edit | Select All.

5. Drag the selected images to the Storyboard or Timeline. The result for the Storyboard is shown in Figure 10-3.

Importing music and narration is achieved in the same manner, by clicking Import Audio Or Music in the Movie Tasks pane. You'll want to have some experience with Movie Maker 2 if you plan to do this. You can add both music and narration, or only narration, or only music. If you decide to narrate your photomontage, you need to verify that your microphone is plugged in and working, and then work through a few steps to record your audio.

Once you have your images in the correct order and your audio added (and any transitions and/or effects applied), you're ready to create the montage. In reality, this is a movie.

FIGURE 10-3 Add images to Storyboard or Timeline

1. If you have a Pocket PC, connect it to the USB port (or appropriate port) on your computer and verify that it is recognized.

2. In Movie Maker 2, in the Movie Tasks pane, under Finish Movie, select Save To My Computer. (If you plan to e-mail it, choose Send In E-Mail instead and work through the wizard.)

3. In the Save Movie Wizard, name the movie appropriately. Choose where on your hard drive to save the file and make a note of the location. Click Next.

4. If you plan to save the movie to your Pocket PC, click the Other Settings radio button, as shown in Figure 10-4, and select from the drop-down list the choice that best matches your Pocket PC's hardware and software. The higher the choice for Kbps, the higher the quality and larger the file. Click Next.

5. If you plan to save the movie to your hard drive, choose Best Quality Playback On My Computer (Recommended). Click Next.

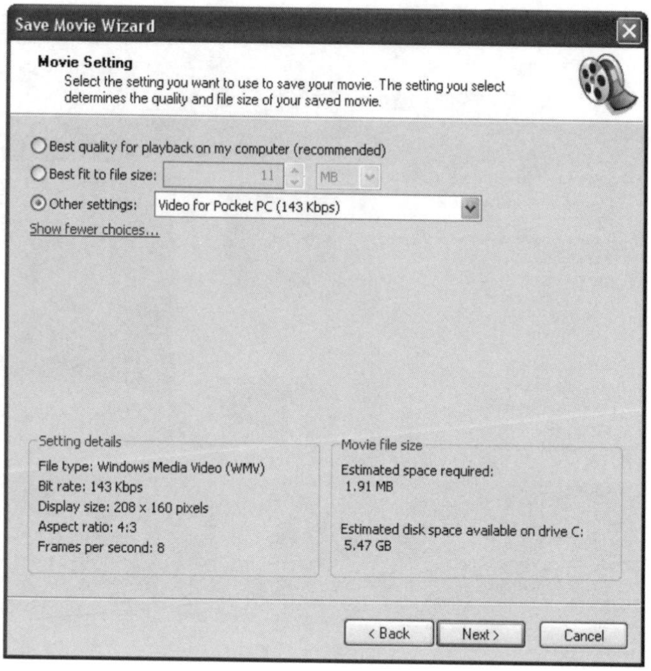

Save Movie Wizard

Movie Setting
Select the setting you want to use to save your movie. The setting you select determines the quality and file size of your saved movie.

○ Best quality for playback on my computer (recommended)
○ Best fit to file size: 11   MB
⊙ Other settings: Video for Pocket PC (143 Kbps)
Show fewer choices...

Setting details
File type: Windows Media Video (WMV)
Bit rate: 143 Kbps
Display size: 208 x 160 pixels
Aspect ratio: 4:3
Frames per second: 8

Movie file size
Estimated space required:
1.91 MB

Estimated disk space available on drive C:
5.47 GB

< Back   Next >   Cancel

FIGURE 10-4 Make the appropriate file type choice

6. Wait while the movie is created. After it is created, close Movie Maker 2.

7. Locate the movie on your hard drive and drag it to your Pocket PC's icon in My Computer. You can also burn the movie to a CD by dragging it to your CD-R or CD-RW drive.

8. The movie will be played on your Pocket PC in Windows Media Player.

 You can play the slideshow saved to your hard drive on your own PC by double-clicking it. It will open and play in Windows Media Player.

You may want to play the movie on your PC before transferring it to the Pocket PC. If the movie isn't what you'd hoped for, you'll have to open the project again and edit that; you can't edit a movie once it's been created. If you decide to edit the project file and create another movie, make sure you delete the unwanted movie file from your hard drive. Otherwise, you'll have a whole slew of files you don't want or need taking up valuable hard drive space.

WINDOWS MEDIA PLAYER

Windows Media Player is the application that ships with Windows XP for playing music and video. It opens automatically when you choose to play either music or a video. When connected to the Internet, Windows Media Player even retrieves information about currently playing media automatically. In this section, you learn how to have more fun with Windows Media Player, including how to edit the data that's retrieved and how to add your own. You'll also learn how to personalize the Media Player so that it works for you, and not the other way around.

  Windows Media Player has been updated several times. The version that ships with Windows XP isn't the latest. If you start Windows Media Player and see a message that an update is available, by all means get it. You can also check for updates from Help | Check For Player Updates. In this section, I'll be using Windows Media Player 10.

⬇ Edit Media Player Metadata

Personalize, add, and replace song lyrics, titles, cover art, and other album information when it is missing, incomplete, or incorrect.

10

When listening to music tracks with Windows Media Player, you have the option to view information about the track, the artist, and the album. You can even view the album's cover art or lyrics if the information is available. This information is obtained automatically if you are online and if Windows Media Player can access the data from one of its databases (hosted by WindowsMedia.com).

Some tracks and albums have quite a bit of data available; others have none or very little. The latter is especially true if you are playing a track or album you created yourself with your own band, or if the music is from a new or obscure band that few people have heard of. In addition, some tracks or albums may simply have wrong or outdated information, or maybe you have the inside scoop on the band and have some inside information currently unavailable online.

When this happens, you can edit and/or add the appropriate data to Windows Media Player yourself, and make it available each time you play the song. You can add or edit to your heart's content, and change virtually any data associated with a track or album. Editing the information isn't just cosmetic, though; when you create auto playlists, the information that Windows Media Player finds is what it uses. If a song is categorized in the wrong genre, for instance, that song will never play when an auto playlist is created and played for that variety of music.

To input information into Windows Media Player that you deem correct, including items that are missing:

1. Open Windows Media Player from Start | All Programs | Accessories | Entertainment | Windows Media Player.

2. Click the Library tab. (In other versions, click the Media Library tab.)

3. Locate a song in which data needs to be changed, either from a playlist, an album, a composer, a genre, or any other category available.

4. Right-click the track and select Find Album Info. Make sure you're connected to the Internet.

5. Read the information offered. To edit any information, click Edit, shown in the lower center of Figure 10-5. (Depending on the song selected, you may also be offered Edit Track Information.)

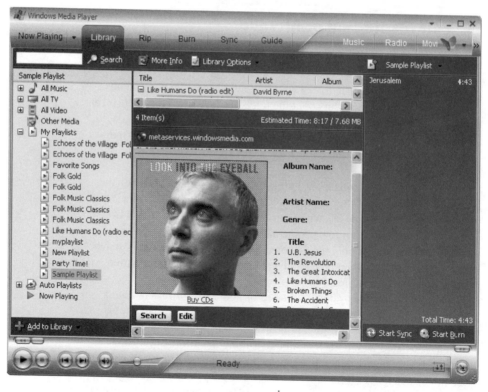

FIGURE 10-5 Windows Media Player 10 offers an Edit option.

6. Make changes as desired. Click Next when complete. Click Finish.

You can also edit using the Advanced Tag Editor. Just right-click any song and choose Advanced Tag Editor. In the Advanced Tag Editor dialog box, shown in Figure 10-6, you can make changes to genre, track titles, track numbers, album name, artist information, lyrics, and more.

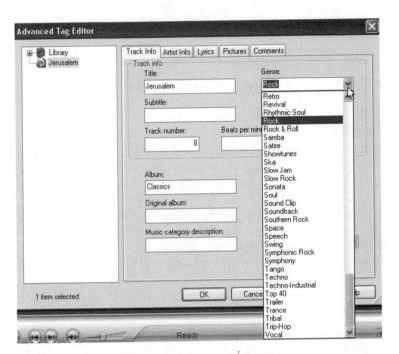

FIGURE 10-6 The Advanced Tag Editor and genre choices

There are many other ways to edit what's shown in Windows Media Player. In the next section, you'll learn one more way.

Use Ratings to Create Personalized Playlists

You can apply ratings to songs to create playlists that are automatically created based on your likes and dislikes.

By default, each time you add a song to the Media Library, it's automatically assigned a rating of three stars. These assigned ratings change automatically based on how often you play the song; that's all integrated into the Media Player. Using the ratings, you can create auto playlists that change as often as your tastes in music do. However, you don't have to be stuck with the automatic ratings given to songs, or wait for the Media Player to update them after you have or have not listened to them the required number of times. You can rate songs yourself.

To rate any song:

1. Open Windows Media Player and click the Library tab (or Media Library tab).

2. Select the song(s) to rate, right-click, and point to Rate Selected Items.

3. Select a rating for the song(s). You'll have choices ranging from one star to five stars.

While this isn't a difficult concept, the things you can do with your assigned ratings can be quite complex. As an example, you can classify your star rating system to mean something other than how much you like or dislike a song. You can use the star ratings to denote specific categories of music, such as music that you play when you have a party or when you're working. You can then use your personalized rating system to create innovative playlists. (Once you've rated a song, the rating overrides any rating that Windows Media Player would ever apply.)

Here is an example of a possible star rating system you could use:

- **One star**   Music that you go to sleep to, soft rock, or music that relaxes.

- **Two stars**   Music that you can listen to while you work, while cleaning the house, or when guests are present and you need a little background music.

- **Three stars**   Music that you listen to often, your favorite tracks, and music you wake up to.

- **Four stars**   Music that you play at parties, dance to, or put on when singing karaoke with friends.

- **Five stars**   Music that is hardcore, metal, grunge, or rap.

You can also create ratings if you are a professional (or wannabe) DJ, by rating music by genres such as music that is suitable for wedding receptions, funerals, graduation parties, birthday parties, and similar gatherings. Once you've rated your songs, creating an auto playlist based on those songs is easy:

1. Open Windows Media Player, choose the Library tab, and select Auto Playlists.

2. Right-click Auto Playlists and select New.

3. In the New Auto Playlist dialog box, shown in Figure 10-7, name the new playlist.

4. Under Music In My Library, click <Click Here To Add Criteria>. Select Auto Rating.

5. Select the new entry, Is At Least, and set the criteria. In Figure 10-7, the criteria has been set to Auto Rating Is 3 Stars. Click OK when finished.

FIGURE 10-7 The New Auto Playlist offers an auto rating choice.

PERFORMANCE AND SECURITY

Windows Media Player's performance and security can be enhanced. Windows Media Player 10 will drag along, hang up, and even close unexpectedly if the computer is bogged down with other tasks. CD and DVD burning software might create a coaster out of your recordable CD and DVD if you listen to streaming video or edit a picture while burning it. To get the most from Windows Media Player, you have to know how to tweak it for best performance. You'll learn some ways in this section.

Securing the Media Player is important, too. This might not ever cross your mind until you find that your kids have made their way into your media library and have watched your R-rated DVDs! Instead of waiting for that to happen, you can set parental controls on your DVDs. You also can take steps to protect the identity of yourself and your family while using Windows Media Player online.

⬇ Common Sense Tricks for Better Performance

Make sure your computer isn't bogged down with other tasks while you're using the Media Player.

One of the major reasons computers have problems and perform poorly is that they simply have too much to do. Themes and screen savers that use system resources, and programs and files that take up valuable hard drive space, can cause performance problems. When cleaning up your computer to enhance performance (refer to Chapter 1), make sure you've dealt with these things appropriately. Turn off themes and system-intensive screen savers that require computations or lots of video memory, uninstall programs you don't need and no longer use, and rid your hard drive of unnecessary files.

Another reason media hangs up, freezes, or performs poorly is that the application, in this case Windows Media Player 10, needs all of the resources it can get its hands on. If the application needs RAM, and you're using what available RAM you have to print a large document or perform a complicated edit in Photoshop, performance will certainly suffer. Use a little common sense; don't try to render a movie while at the same time you're burning a DVD, and make sure your applications are getting the attention they need from both RAM and the processor.

You can also enhance computer, and thus media, performance by making sure you don't have unnecessary programs running in the background that you don't know about or need. If you've downloaded a lot of programs, shareware, freeware, or third-party applications from the Internet, chances are you're going to be more than a little surprised at what you find running behind the scenes.

You can use the System Configuration Utility to see what is running in the background. To open this utility:

1. Click Start | Run and, in the Run dialog box, type **msconfig.exe**.

2. Click the Startup tab and scroll down to the bottom of the list, as shown in Figure 10-8.

3. Uncheck items you no longer use. In Figure 10-8, I've unchecked, among others, TrayMinimizer and Wallpaper Changer, two PowerToy programs I tried; Emomail, a third-party e-mailing program; and TweakMaster, a shareware program that has expired. You can keep items you want, though; I've kept FullShot 7, and msnmsgr (MSN Messenger).

4. Click OK and restart the computer.

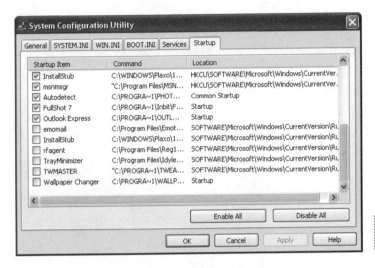

FIGURE 10-8 Disable unwanted programs

If you're ever unsure about what an item does, a quick search on Google for the entry will generally produce results. Searching for one entry on my computer, SisUSBrg, Google offered up information that this particular entry is a sound-card driver. It would make sense that this is a necessary component.

When removing items, choose the items one at a time, restart the computer, and verify that you don't get any error messages. If the computer runs fine, return here and delete another.

 Don't uninstall anything you aren't familiar with. Windows XP needs RUNDLL32, for instance. Only uninstall what you recognize and know you don't need.

You're the Parent

If you don't want your kids watching what you watch and viewing what you view, set parental controls.

If you have Windows user accounts and passwords set up for everyone who accesses your computer, you can use the DVD ratings included on DVD disks to control which users can access and watch what DVDs. The Motion Picture Association of America rates DVDs as G, PG, PG-13, R, NC-17, and Not Rated. If you set parental controls, anything that is rated higher than what you specify won't be played unless the viewer has a valid administrator account and password.

To enable parental controls in Windows Media Player:

1. Open Windows Media Player. Right-click the title bar, point to Tools, and click Options.

2. In the Options dialog box, click the DVD tab.

3. Check the Parental Control box, and then select a rating, as shown in Figure 10-9.

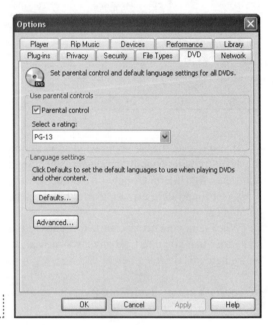

FIGURE 10-9 Set parental controls

4. Click OK.

⬎ Protect Your Identity

Don't let your identity go unprotected.

Windows Media Player is pretty secure as is, and before you start worrying about online identity theft, I want to clarify that the Media Player never sends anyone any *personally identifiable information* about you to any web sites it visits. However, some information is sent out to the Internet when you're logged on and using Windows Media Player, and you should know what it is.

When playing CDs and DVDs while online, Windows Media Player connects to the Internet and returns information about the media you're playing, such as the songs included on the CD, album cover art, artist information, DVD information, and more. However, Microsoft doesn't know what music you listen to or what videos you download and watch. For those who are not completely reassured by that statement and want to feel even more secure, I've included this section.

You can configure the options to be a little stricter than those set by default. Doing so will allow you to have a say in exactly what (if any) information is sent to Microsoft or any third-party music sites. To see your privacy options and perhaps change them:

1. Open Windows Media Player, right-click the title bar, and choose Tools | Options.

2. Click the Privacy tab. One of the options is Send Unique Player ID To Content Providers. Information it sends isn't personally identifiable, but it may send information about connection time, IP address, OS version, Media Player version, player identification number, date, protocol, and so forth. The purpose of this, of course, is to provide your content provider with information that will help it serve you better and give you a better experience and higher-quality output. However, if sending this information seems intrusive, you can disable it. Figure 10-10 shows the options.

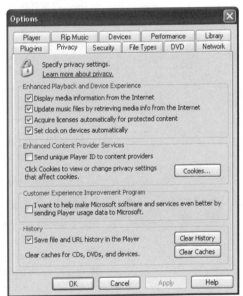

3. Another option that you can disable is Update Music Files By Retrieving Media Info From The Internet. When this is checked, and it is by default, the Media Player will attempt to obtain information about your CDs and DVDs from WindowsMedia.com, including artist name, track name, and similar data. Information about your music will be gathered and sent to a database, for the purpose of enhancing your musical experience. If you do not want to share information about your CDs and DVDs, and you do not want to obtain information from WindowsMedia.com, uncheck this box.

FIGURE 10-10 The Privacy tab offers personalization options for the Media Player.

10

4. If you ever want to clear Media Player's History, click Clear History on the Privacy tab.

5. To clear caches for CDs, DVDs, and devices, click Clear Caches.

BACK UP YOUR MEDIA

As mentioned several times throughout this book, backing up data is extremely important. You know you should back up your important files regularly, and that includes your pictures, music, and videos. Many people simply drag and drop the folders to an external drive or use CD burning software to burn their data to CDs. Unfortunately, this way of backing up leaves you wide open for procrastinating, and many times, the job simply isn't done.

Windows XP Professional contains a backup utility that can help you in your quest for regular backups. Windows Backup Utility helps you back up automatically, and on a schedule. And, although it doesn't let you burn to CDs, there are ways around that, making the Backup Utility the perfect option for those who need a little reminder every week. If you have Windows XP Home, you can still use the Backup Utility, you just have to install it.

◥ Using Windows Backup Utility in Windows XP Home

If you have Windows XP Home, you're probably wondering where the Backup Utility is; follow the steps here to install it.

The Backup Utility that is native to Windows XP Professional isn't included by default in Windows XP Home Edition. If you have the Home Edition, you'll have to take some steps to install it manually.

If you have Windows XP Home and the Windows XP Home Edition CD-ROM (not a restore CD):

1. Place the Windows XP Home Edition CD-ROM into the CD-ROM drive.

2. When the program opens, click Exit.

3. Open My Computer and locate the CD drive.

4. Right-click the drive's icon and click Explore.

5. Open the VALUEADD folder.

6. Open the MSFT folder, and then NTBACKUP.

7. Double-click the Ntbackup.msi file and work through the wizard. When complete, click Finish.

➘ Creating a Backup for Media Only

The Backup Utility can be used to create various types of backups,
including one just for media.

While full backups can be quite useful, sometimes you just need to back
up your media files. When creating this type of backup, you browse to all
of your media files, no matter where they are stored, and select them for
backup. The files don't have to be on only one drive, and they can be backed
up from Network Places. Once you configure the backup, you can schedule
it to run at a time that's convenient for you.

To create a backup for media only:

1. Open the Backup Utility, located in the All Programs | Accessories |
   System Tools list. By default, it opens in Wizard Mode. For the
   purposes of creating the type of media backup you want to create
   here, you should start the program in Advanced Mode. If a wizard
   starts, close it. Figure 10-11 shows what the interface should
   look like.

FIGURE 10-11   Backing up media in Advanced Mode

10

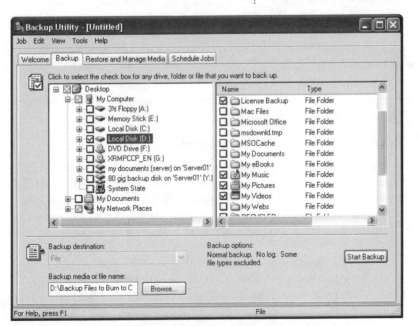

2. Once in Advanced Mode, choose the Backup tab. From here, you can create a backup that is specific only to the media stored on your computer. Expand each drive and locate and check all folders that contain media.

3. For the Backup Media Or File Name box located at the bottom of the Backup tab, click Browse and locate a place to permanently or temporarily store the backup. Later, you can drag and drop the file to another drive or to a CD or DVD.

4. Click Start Backup, read the choices, and click Start Backup again. You'll need to make a choice about the type of backup based on whether you prefer to create a new backup each time or append the data to the old backup. I prefer to create a new backup each time, but it takes longer.

5. Once the backup is created, you can save it as a job for future use. Click Job | Save Selection As. Name the selection **Media**.

 The next time you want to run the job manually, click Job | Media.bks, the saved selection in Step 5.

Keeping your backups on an external hard drive is a pretty safe way to keep them. That is, until there's a fire or flood, in which case having saved them to a CD and put them in another room or home may avoid some additional anguish. To burn to a CD, simply locate the backup and drag and drop it to your CD-R or DVD burner. If there's ever a disaster, you'll be glad you did.

◥ Creating a Schedule

Scheduling backups is one way to make sure it gets done.

One of the best ways to guarantee you'll remember to create regular backups is to schedule them. In this case, you want to create a schedule for the saved job just created, which you named Media. Scheduling backups is achieved using a wizard, and the wizard walks you through all required steps.

To use the wizard to create a scheduled backup for the latest job, Media:

1. Open the Backup Utility, located in the All Programs | Accessories | System Tools list. By default, it opens in Wizard Mode. As in the prior section, for the purposes of creating the type of media backup you want to create here, start the program in Advanced Mode. If a wizard starts, close it. Figure 10-11 in the prior section shows what the interface should look like.

2. Once in Advanced Mode, choose the Backup tab.

3. Click Job | Media.bks, the job created in the last section. If you did not create a job, select the folders that contain media to back up.

4. Click the Schedule Jobs tab.

5. Select Add Job, and click Yes to use the files currently open.

6. Click Next to start the wizard, and click Next again to accept the selected files and folders. Choose a place to save your backup and create a name for it. Click Browse to choose a location, and click Open when you have found the location. Figure 10-12 shows the results of these actions. Click Next.

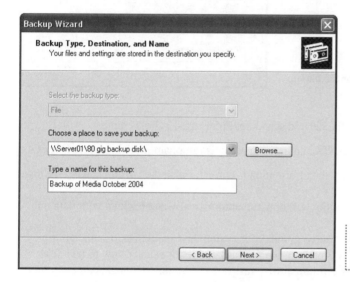

FIGURE 10-12 Tell the wizard where to save the files and what to name them

7. On the Type Of Backup page, select Normal. Click Next. (For more information about types of backups, see the Help files.)

8. On the How To Back Up page, check Verify Data After Backup. Leave the other boxes unchecked. Click Next.

9. On the Backup Options page, choose to append the data to an existing backup or create a new backup and replace the old one. I prefer the latter. Click Next.

10. On the When To Back Up page, select Later, name the job, and click Set Schedule. Figure 10-13 shows the Schedule Job options.

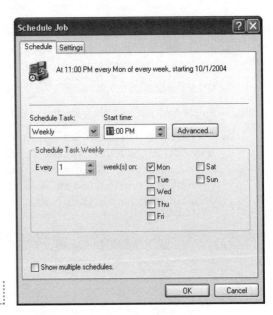

FIGURE 10-13 Set a schedule for the backup

11. Set the desired schedule. Figure 10-13 shows mine.

12. Click OK and input an administrator name and password. Click OK.

13. Verify the information is correct, finish the wizard, and click Close.

The Backup Utility will now run automatically and back up your data on a schedule.

Now that you've gotten your system and media performance in tip-top shape, it's time to move forward and learn exactly how to be a true administrator. Administrative tasks, if you're one to tweak, can be quite interesting. In the next chapter you'll learn some of my favorites, including setting up auditing of events, managing users and groups, configuring a local security policy, and viewing in-depth system information. These tasks can really get your computer secure and keep it that way—and that's security from your kids, unintentional harm from visitors, and even from your spouse!

CHAPTER 11
BUILT-IN UTILITIES AND ADMINISTRATIVE TOOLS

Windows XP Professional comes with lots of administrative tools and built-in utilities, but only a few of these utilities are available in Windows XP Home. That's because XP Professional is the edition used by small businesses and large corporations who need the added functionality. The administrative options in Windows XP Professional give administrators more control over the operating system, allow them to create and control users and groups, and let them monitor who logs on and when. These options also allow administrators to log security events and other activities, and limit what happens if a user types in the wrong password a predetermined number of times. Because home users don't generally need this functionality, Windows XP Home does not include all of it.

If multiple users access your computer, if your computer is in a public place, if your computer is not secure at night (perhaps a cleaning crew comes in), or if you have family members or guests you don't want accessing your computer, you may want to consider upgrading so that you can have these added features.

In this final chapter, I'll discuss some of the tools and built-in utilities, some available in both XP Home and XP Professional, and others only available in XP Professional, including those that enable you to create groups of users, assign permissions and manage shares, take advantage of security auditing and make sense of the logs, configure password requirements and create their security rules, and acquire in-depth system information.

MANAGING USERS AND GROUPS

If multiple users access a single computer, which might occur in a business or a large household, you may want to assign your users to a group and manage the group as one unit, instead of managing each user separately. Managing a group of ten users is far more efficient than managing those ten users independently. With a group, you have to assign permissions, rights, and rules only once, not ten times. It's also easier to add a member to the group, as any member in the group is assigned the same permissions and rights as all the other members automatically. It's a one-stop-administrating experience.

⬎ Create a Group
Administering a group of users is easier and more efficient than administering each user independently.

To create a group, you first need to have a few users. Users can be created in User Accounts, accessed through Control Panel. Once you have created multiple users, you can add them to a group for easy administration.

There are several built-in groups you can choose from, or you can create your own. Each of the built-in groups already has specific permissions applied to it. For example, members of the Power Users group can create user accounts, create local groups, and add or remove users from groups. Members of the Guests group cannot do any of these things. There are also built-in groups for administrators, backup operators, and general users. In this section, though, you'll create an entirely new group.

 The Help and Support Files offer lots of information about built-in groups and their permissions.

To create a new group and add users:

1. Right-click My Computer and click Manage.

2. In the Computer Management console, expand Local Users And Groups. Click Users to see all of the users created on the computer. You may see users you didn't create, and that's normal. The Help Assistant is considered a user, as are others. Ignore extraneous user accounts that you did not create.

3. Click Groups to see the built-in groups already created, as shown in Figure 11-1. You can add users to any of these groups or create your own. Built-in groups have specific permissions and rights already assigned to them.

11

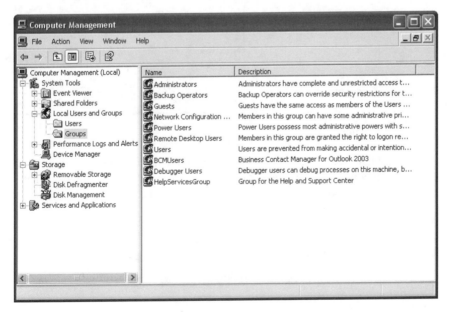

FIGURE 11-1 There are several built-in groups you can add users to.

4. To create a new group, right-click Group in the left pane and click New Group.

5. In the New Group dialog box, create a group name and description.

6. Click Add.

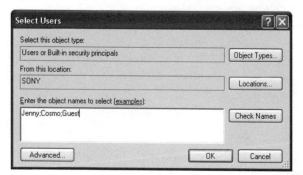

7. In the Select Users dialog box, enter the user account names for the members to add. Separate members by semicolons. Figure 11-2 shows an example.

8. Click Check Names. The names will be automatically formatted using the syntax necessary. Click OK. Figure 11-3 shows the resulting group.

FIGURE 11-2 Choose who will be in the group

FIGURE 11-3 A new group with three members

9. Click OK.

When you add users to a built-in group, that group takes on the permissions already assigned to that group, as mentioned before. But what about groups you create? That's a little different. Permissions for groups you've created are detailed in the next section.

↘ May I Have Permission, Please?

Newly created groups already have permissions assigned to them, but what are they?

Members you add to groups you create already have permissions assigned to them, because they are automatically assigned to the generic group, Users, also. By default, members of Users, and thus the members in your new group, already have specific permissions and can already perform specific tasks.

Members of the Users group and any personalized group you create can do the following:

■ Run applications installed on the computer

■ Use all printers connected to the computer or the network

■ Turn off the computer

■ Lock a workstation

■ Create their own local groups

■ Modify the groups they've created

■ Remove a laptop from a docking station

However, members cannot share directories or share printers.

Although I don't suggest that you do this, only because it complicates troubleshooting when things go awry, it's certainly possible to change what any built-in group or any group you've created can and can't do, by changing the default permissions in the Local Security Policy console. For instance, only members of the Administrator group can change the system time, back up files and directories, install device drivers, manage an auditing or security log, restore files and directories, and perform a myriad of other tasks. However, if you need your newly created group members to have permission to back up and restore files, you can certainly make that change. On the reverse side of that, members of your group can perform tasks you may not want them to be able to, such as undocking a computer or shutting it down. You can change this behavior too.

To change the default permissions for your group or any other:

1. Open Control Panel | Administrative Tools | Local Security Policy.

2. Expand Local Policies and select User Rights Assignment to locate the item to change. Figure 11-4 shows an example.

3. In the right pane, locate the particular policy to change, and double-click it to open its Properties dialog box.

4. To add a group and allow a policy, click Add User Or Group. To remove a group and disallow the policy, click Remove. In Figure 11-5, I'll click Add User Or Group, and add my newly created group. Members of that group will then be able to back up files and directories as needed.

5. Click OK when complete and close the Local Security Settings console.

11

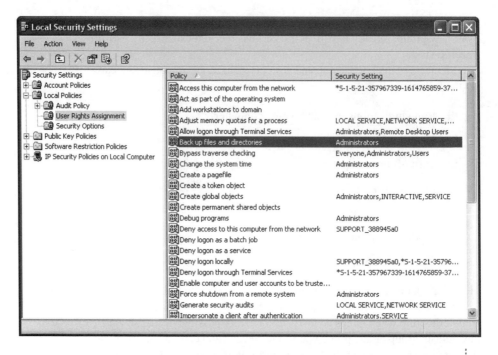

FIGURE 11-4 Locate the policy to change for a specific group or to add a group who can perform it

FIGURE 11-5 Adding a group enables the members of the group to perform the task.

◥ Manage Shared Files and Folders

*Your shared folders can be intricately managed; specific groups can
be allowed or disallowed access to them.*

When Simple File Sharing is turned off, as
detailed in Chapter 8, you can use the groups you've
created to help protect the shared files and folders
on your computer. As a small business owner, this
might mean allowing general employees access to
specific folders that contain the data they need, while
not allowing them to access the company's profit and
loss statements. You can manage the latter by only
allowing administrators access. As a mother or father,
you can add your kids to groups with limited access.
You can then configure this group to allow access to
the shared folders of pictures and music, but not to
the shared folder that contains videos.

To allow or disallow a specific group access to
a shared folder:

1. Right-click the shared folder to amend and
   choose Sharing And Security.

2. Verify that Share This Folder is selected and
   a share name is configured. Click Permissions.

3. In the Permissions dialog box, shown in
   Figure 11-6, select the Everyone group and
   then click Remove. To intricately manage this
   folder, you cannot allow "everyone" access to it.

4. To add a specific group, click Add.

5. In the Select Users And Groups dialog box,
   type the names of the groups to add. Only
   members in the groups added can access
   the folder once this is done. Separate group
   names with a semicolon. Click Check Names,
   and then click OK.

6. Back in the Permissions dialog box, select
   your group and look at the default permissions.
   Change them as desired. Figure 11-7 shows an
   example.

7. Click OK. Click OK again to close the
   Properties dialog box.

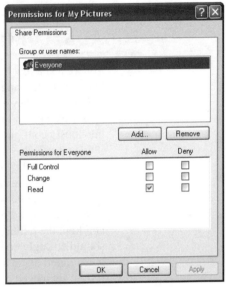

FIGURE 11-6 Remove the Everyone group
if you want to intricately manage the folder

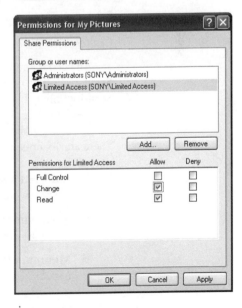

FIGURE 11-7 New groups are configured

11

You can also set advanced security options from the Security tab, available in the shared file's Properties dialog box. You saw this tab and this dialog box during Step 2 earlier. For more information, view the Help and Support files.

LOCAL SECURITY POLICY

You've had a few lessons in local security policies throughout this book, but none addressing logon and password security. These are called *account policies*, and they allow administrators to create rules for users regarding password age and length, complexity, and whether or not users can use previously configured passwords. Administrators can also decide what to do if and when a user has a specific number of failed logon attempts, including whether or not they will be locked out of the computer and, if so, for how long.

These policies are not set by default. If multiple users access the computer and you want passwords to be as secure as possible, consider creating password policies. If the computer is available to cleaning crews, children, the public, employees, or strangers when you aren't around, you should strongly consider creating policies that address account lockout when failed logon attempts are made. A would-be hacker won't get very far if they get locked out for an hour after three failed logon attempts. And, if a user really does forget the password, you can reset it quickly.

⊌ Configure Password Requirements

Complex passwords help secure the computer for everyone who uses it.

All account policies are set in Local Security Policy. To locate Local Security Policy, open Control Panel | Administrative Tools | Local Security Policy. In the Local Security Settings dialog box, expand Account Policies and select Password Policy.

To set any policy, simply double-click it and make the changes desired. There are six options in a workgroup, but only five relate to workgroups:

- **Enforce Password History**   With this enabled, users cannot use old passwords (up to the last 24).

- **Maximum Password Age**   With this enabled, users must change their password after a specific number of days.

- **Minimum Password Age**   With this enabled, users must wait a specific number of days before changing their password.

■ **Minimum Password Length**   Specifies how long the password
  must be.

■ **Password Must Meet Complexity Requirements**   Requires users
  to create passwords that contain at least six characters, upper- and
  lowercase letters, at least one number, and a nonalphanumeric
  character, such as a question mark.

Each of these policies can be created independently. You can have
a maximum password age for instance, without requiring the password to
be complex. You can decide just how secure you want users' passwords to be.

⬎ Configure Account Lockout

*Keep hackers from logging on by locking the user out after a specific
number of failed logon attempts.*

There are only three account lockout policies, and all have to do with
how many times a user can attempt to log on, and what happens after that
threshold is met. For instance, you can configure account lockout policies
so that after a person attempts to log on three times, they are locked out from
logging on for 30 minutes. After 30 minutes, the user can attempt to log on
again. If a user has forgotten his password, he'll have to come to you, an
administrator, to let him log on again. You'll have to reset his password.

As with configuring password policies, you set account lockout policies
by double-clicking the policy to change. Unlike password policies, though,
which are independent, account lockout policies are dependent. If you
configure account lockout after three failed attempts, you must define
what will happen after the lockout occurs. For that reason, it's best to step
through the procedure systematically:

1. Open Control Panel | Administrative
   Tools | Local Security Policy.

2. In the Local Security Settings dialog
   box, expand Account Policies and select
   Account Lockout Policy.

3. In the right pane, double-click Account
   Lockout Threshold to open the dialog
   box shown in Figure 11-8. Choose how
   many attempts a user can make to log
   on before being locked out, and then
   click OK.

FIGURE 11-8 Configure logon attempts

4. Click OK to accept the default options for lockout duration and resetting the account, each of which is 30 minutes.

5. To make any changes to the time limits set as defaults, double-click Account Lockout Duration. Set a new time and click OK. Repeat for Reset Account Lockout Counter After, if desired.

If a user has forgotten her password and cannot log on after several attempts, you'll have to reset the password. Resetting a password is achieved through the Computer Management console:

1. Right-click My Computer and click Manage.

2. Expand Local Users And Groups and select Users.

3. Select the user who is locked out and double-click to open that user's Properties dialog box.

4. Check User Must Change Password At Next Logon, and then click OK. Uncheck Password Never Expires, Account Is Disabled, and Account Is Locked Out if any are checked. Click OK.

EVENT VIEWER

Now that you have completely revamped how users obtain access to files and folders, and how they log on, it's time to see if those users are following the rules accordingly. With security logging and auditing, you can see what's going on at your computer when you aren't there.

Using Event Viewer, another application in Control Panel's Administrative Tools, you can see successful and failed logon attempts, successful and failed attempts to make policy changes, and successful and failed attempts to use privileges.

 Windows XP Home Edition also collects this information.

 ## See What's Happening When You're Not Around

Auditing lets you see what's going on when you're not around, including who successfully logs on and who doesn't.

To get the most from Event Viewer and its log of security events, you need to open Event Viewer, do a little tweaking, and then decide what events matter most to you. In general, logon events are a good category to watch, because several failed attempts in the middle of the night might show that your janitorial staff is a little too nosy. You might also look for failed policy changes, indicating some larger problem with policies or the system itself.

You'll also want to decide what to do when the event log is full. You can either overwrite the oldest events or clear the log manually. The former is usually the better choice, as you may not view events as often as you should, and manual deletion requires additional work (and a good memory). You can also configure exactly what to log—successes, failures, or both. Usually both is fine, and is the default.

To open Event Viewer, view events, change views, and configure what is audited by default:

1. Open Control Panel | Administrative Tools | Event Viewer.

2. Select Security, as shown in Figure 11-9. Scroll to see both successes and failures.

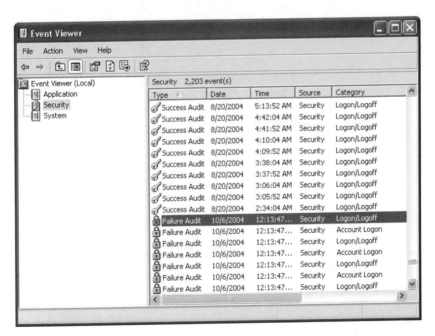

FIGURE 11-9 Failures need to be looked into to determine whether security is at risk.

3. To sort events by successes and failures, click Type. To sort events by date, click Date. To sort events by category, click Category. Use the same procedure for the additional headings.

4. To change what's being audited from successes and failures to either or none at all, right-click Security and click Properties.

5. In the Security Properties dialog box, shown in Figure 11-10, click the General tab. Here, you can decide how to manage the logs—manually or automatically. You can also increase the size of the log file.

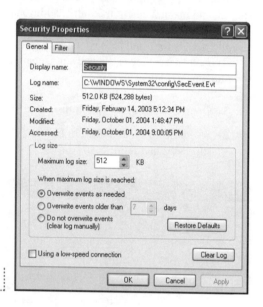

FIGURE 11-10 Configure defaults

6. Click the Filter tab. To change what is audited, check or uncheck Success Audit, Failure Audit, or both. Click OK. Do not close the Event Viewer.

◣ Make Sense of Auditing Logs

So what does all of that mumbo jumbo collected about an event actually mean?

Looking at a failed event's data often won't provide much useful information, although it might if it's a logon event; if it's a policy change event, it likely won't. Sometimes it's difficult to make sense of it all. However, there is more than one way to get the information you need, and Microsoft offers codes for every event and a place to get more information about any event recorded.

Figure 11-11 shows a failed logon attempt. The date was December 15, 2004, it was 10:44 in the morning, and the logon failure is listed as Unknown User Name Or Bad Password. The User Name is Joli Ballew, that's me, and that's about the time I log on to my computer each morning. This particular event does not concern me, as it was likely a typo on my part.

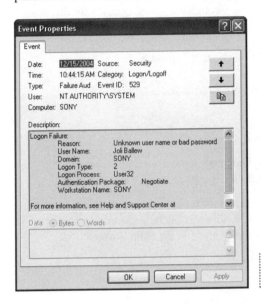

FIGURE 11-11 Not all failed logon attempts are security threats.

The next sample event, shown in Figure 11-12, is a little disconcerting. It says the logon attempt was made by Microsoft_Authentication_Package_ V1_0, and there's an error code. It also says I can get more information by clicking the link to Microsoft offered. That's usually a good choice if you see something out of the ordinary. Although I trust Microsoft, I'm just not sure what this is.

11

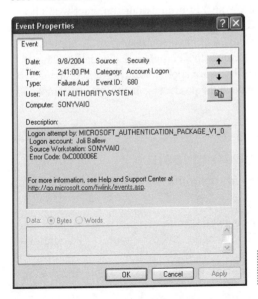

FIGURE 11-12 Some events are hard to diagnose.

After accessing the link and reading the information, I find that a set of credentials was passed to the authentication system by a local process, a remote process, or a user. Looking through the various causes for this error, I can presume an incorrect password was entered. At 2:41 P.M., that's likely the case.

You can get more information about any event easily:

1. Open Control Panel | Administrative Tools | Event Viewer.

2. Click Security.

3. Locate a failed event and double-click it.

4. Read the information given, noting the username, time, and date. See if there are similar failed events recently.

5. In the Event Properties dialog box, click the link to obtain more information. Read the data offered, matching the error codes, if applicable, to the error codes given in the Help files.

6. Click OK when finished.

SYSTEM INFORMATION

There are a couple of places to get information about your system when things go wrong, but it's also a good idea to access and print the information when times are good. That way, if you ever have to take your computer to a repair shop or order RAM or a failed part online, you'll be able to put your hands on the information you need quickly, even if your computer won't boot.

In addition to internal hardware, it's also important to know where to find product IDs, product web sites, and phone numbers for the applications you own, just in case you ever have to do a complete reinstallation. This is especially true of shareware and freeware applications, whose companies may be reluctant to let you download the product again. And those companies are often also unreachable.

↘ Get Basic System Diagnostics

Windows XP offers resources for obtaining basic information in its Help and Support files.

If you ever need to know the general specifications of your computer—for instance, the model number, BIOS version, processor type, or IP address—you can get the information quickly from the Help and Support files. My Computer Information, an available option in Help and Support, also offers OS version information, including service packs installed, the speed and version of your processor, and general computer information such as system name, workgroup name, and time zone. This information can come in handy when talking to a technician, or when trying to troubleshoot a computer you're unfamiliar with.

To obtain this information from the Help and Support files:

1. Choose Start | Help And Support.

2. Under Pick A Task, click Use Tools To View Your Computer Information And Diagnose Problems.

3. Under Tools in the left pane, select My Computer Information.

4. In the right pane, select View General System Information About This Computer.

5. Read and/or print the information, and then click Back.

6. In the right pane, select View The Status Of My System Hardware And Software. Figure 11-13 shows a sample report.

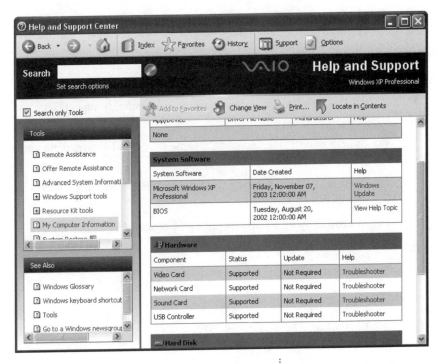

FIGURE 11-13 Sample status report of hardware

You can use the information in the status report to diagnose and repair problems. Specifically, look for obsolete device drivers and for any required updates. Figure 11-13 shows a healthy system.

➘ Get Advanced System Diagnostics

The command-line tool Msinfo32.exe allows you to view advanced system information.

The Help and Support files offer much more system information than introduced in the prior section, and it would behoove you to take a look at what's available, just in case you ever need it. One of the items available is Advanced System Information. You can access the information from Help and Support, although it's easier to get the information via the Run dialog box.

Advanced system information offers just about anything you'd ever need to know about your computer, including the following:

- Basic information about the computer, as offered in the previous section.

- Hardware information, including any conflicts for resources, forced hardware, or memory issues. *Forced hardware* is legacy hardware, such as non-Plug and Play ISA network cards. Older hardware is notorious for causing problems.

- Component information, including multimedia, CD-ROMs, sound devices, displays, modems, network cards, ports, storage, USBs, and problem devices.

- System information, including drivers, signed and unsigned, running tasks, startup programs, and more.

- Internet settings, including versions, connectivity, cache, content, and security.

- Microsoft applications, including Microsoft Office and the applications that ship with it.

To acquire and print this information:

1. Click Start | Run.

2. Type **msinfo32.exe** and click OK.

3. Expand any tree to view its contents. Figure 11-14 shows a sampling.

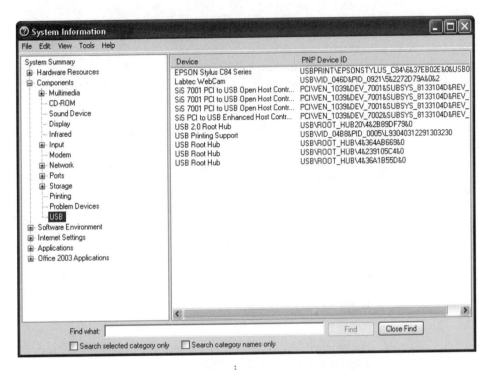

FIGURE 11-14 System Information offers a wealth of data.

11

4. To print the report, choose File | Print.

↘ View Installed Applications' Properties

If you ever have to reinstall your operating system, you'll need the product codes for all of your software handy.

Hopefully, you'll never have a complete meltdown of the operating system. There are always other options to reinstalling the entire OS. You can try System Restore, run **sfc /scannow** at a command prompt, and use the troubleshooting wizards in Help and Support to locate and repair difficult problems with hardware. You can also uninstall and reinstall software if problems arise with a particular application.

However, there may come a time when you will have to do a complete reinstallation, or at least reinstall the software you own. If that happens, you'll have to know each application's product ID, and perhaps the company's phone number and web address. Not all software comes on a CD-ROM with the product ID on the case; quite a bit of software is downloaded from the Internet and IDs are sent via e-mail. If you never burned the program and installation files to a CD yourself, backed them up, or kept a log of product ID numbers, you'll have to download and/or obtain the data again.

So, how do you obtain all the codes and information you'll need for a reinstallation? Well, you have to do a little sleuthing, and be a little pessimistic by preparing for the worst. Here are some places to find product IDs and/or additional information:

- Open Advanced System Information. Product IDs for Microsoft products may be in the trees under Applications or in one marked for a specific program, such as Office 2003 Applications.

- Check for product IDs on CD-ROM cases and accompanying inserts.

- Open each program for which you can't find a product ID and click Help | About This Product (or something similar). The product ID is almost always listed there.

- For programs downloaded from the Internet, choose Help | About This Product (or something similar).

- Some software, such as freeware, won't have a product ID code.

Well, that about wraps it up. By now, your computer should be personalized with pictures and screen savers, tweaked out, and running just the way you want it to. Hopefully, you're using local security policies and administrative tools to keep your computer safe, and maybe you're even giving working at home a shot. Remember to back up regularly, keep your updates coming, and make sure your antivirus software is working properly. Make sure SP2 is downloaded and is configured properly, too, and that your kids are always safe when online. Happy computing and stay tuned for more *Hardcore* books!

Index

INTERNATIONAL CONTACT INFORMATION

AUSTRALIA
McGraw-Hill Book Company
Australia Pty. Ltd.
TEL +61-2-9900-1800
FAX +61-2-9878-8881
http://www.mcgraw-hill.com.au
books-it_sydney@mcgraw-hill.com

CANADA
McGraw-Hill Ryerson Ltd.
TEL +905-430-5000
FAX +905-430-5020
http://www.mcgraw-hill.ca

GREECE, MIDDLE EAST, & AFRICA
(Excluding South Africa)
McGraw-Hill Hellas
TEL +30-210-6560-990
TEL +30-210-6560-993
TEL +30-210-6560-994
FAX +30-210-6545-525

MEXICO (Also serving Latin America)
McGraw-Hill Interamericana Editores
S.A. de C.V.
TEL +525-1500-5108
FAX +525-117-1589
http://www.mcgraw-hill.com.mx
carlos_ruiz@mcgraw-hill.com

SINGAPORE (Serving Asia)
McGraw-Hill Book Company
TEL +65-6863-1580
FAX +65-6862-3354
http://www.mcgraw-hill.com.sg
mghasia@mcgraw-hill.com

SOUTH AFRICA
McGraw-Hill South Africa
TEL +27-11-622-7512
FAX +27-11-622-9045
robyn_swanepoel@mcgraw-hill.com

SPAIN
McGraw-Hill/
Interamericana de España, S.A.U.
TEL +34-91-180-3000
FAX +34-91-372-8513
http://www.mcgraw-hill.es
professional@mcgraw-hill.es

UNITED KINGDOM, NORTHERN,
EASTERN, & CENTRAL EUROPE
McGraw-Hill Education Europe
TEL +44-1-628-502500
FAX +44-1-628-770224
http://www.mcgraw-hill.co.uk
emea_queries@mcgraw-hill.com

ALL OTHER INQUIRIES Contact:
McGraw-Hill/Osborne
TEL +1-510-420-7700
FAX +1-510-420-7703
http://www.osborne.com
omg_international@mcgraw-hill.com

Sound Off!

Visit us at **www.osborne.com/bookregistration** and let us know what you thought of this book. While you're online you'll have the opportunity to register for newsletters and special offers from McGraw-Hill/Osborne.

We want to hear from you!

Sneak Peek

Visit us today at **www.betabooks.com** and see what's coming from McGraw-Hill/Osborne tomorrow!

Based on the successful software paradigm, Bet@Books™ allows computing professionals to view partial and sometimes complete text versions of selected titles online. Bet@Books™ viewing is free, invites comments and feedback, and allows you to "test drive" books in progress on the subjects that interest you the most.

Know How

How to Do Everything with Your Digital Camera
Third Edition
ISBN: 0-07-223081-9

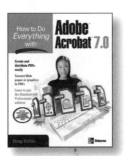

How to Do Everything with Adobe Acrobat 7.0
ISBN: 0-07-225788-1

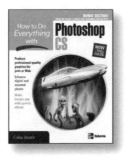

How to Do Everything with Photoshop CS
ISBN: 0-07-223143-2
4-color

How to Do Everything with Windows XP
Third Edition
ISBN: 0-07-225953-1

How to Do Everything with eBay
ISBN: 0-07-225426-2

How to Do Everything with Your eBay Business
Second Edition
ISBN: 0-07-226164-1

How to Do Everything with Your Palm Handheld
Fifth Edition
ISBN: 0-07-225870-5

How to Do Everything with Your iPod & iPod mini
Second Edition
ISBN: 0-07-225452-1

How to Do Everything with Your iMac
4th Edition
ISBN: 0-07-223188-2

How to Do Everything with Your iPAQ Pocket PC
Second Edition
ISBN: 0-07-222950-0

McGraw Hill Osborne
www.osborne.com